Highland Park

1914 Independent School District 2014

Celebrating 100 years of excellence in learning and service

Special Thanks

Our sincere thanks go to Allie Beth and Pierce Allman for their generous underwriting of this book. The Allmans are longtime civic leaders and enthusiastic supporters of Highland Park ISD and the Park Cities community. They have generously given their time and expertise to help guide the district's centennial celebration. Pierce is a 1950 graduate of Highland Park High School and was honored as a Distinguished Alumnus in 2012. It is evident that the Allmans have a special place in their hearts for our schools, students and staff, and we have a special place in our heart for them as well.

In gratitude,

The Highland Park ISD Board of Trustees, Superintendent Dr. Dawson Orr & staff

Allie Beth Allman
& Associates
Local. Real Estate. Leaders.

Highland Park Independent School District
7015 Westchester Dr.
Dallas, TX 75205

Published in cooperation with
Reedy Press
PO Box 5131
St. Louis, MO 63139

Library of Congress Control Number: 2014910433

ISBN: 9781935806080

Printed in the United States of America

14 15 16 17 18   5 4 3 2 1

In gathering 100 years of history, a great effort has been made to ensure the accuracy of information and the proper identification of photos. However, in any undertaking of this size and scope, we acknowledge that errors and omissions may occur. If you notice any errors, please let us know by emailing hponline@hpisd.org so that we may update our archives and make corrections for use in future publications.

Front and back cover photos by David Leeson

Contents

Acknowledgements

This 100–year history was a labor of love. It began decades ago when unofficial historians took it upon themselves to document the stories of our schools, our students, and all those who support the learning that takes place every day in our classrooms.

For example, in 1974, Armstrong Elementary music teacher Vernelle Stimson assembled a priceless scrapbook entitled *The First 60 Years of Armstrong Elementary*. Considering that Armstrong was the first school in the district and the only school for the first eight years, she had a lot of territory to cover, and she did so in a meticulous and thoughtful manner.

We also drew upon some more official documents and sources, including the following:

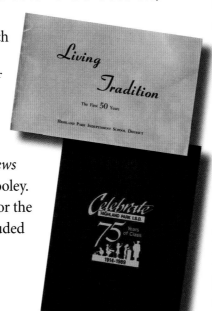

- *Living Tradition: The First 50 Years*, which marked HPISD's 50th birthday
- *Celebrate Highland Park ISD: 75 Years of Class*, a booklet authored by Diane Galloway and Bill Crook
- A 100–year history of HPISD, which was written by *The Dallas Morning News* columnist and local historian Kirk Dooley. This account provided the first draft for the decade–by–decade glance that is included in this book.
- *Highlander* yearbooks
- *The Bagpipe* archives
- *The Dallas Morning News* archives

Thank you to Mr. Dooley and Mrs. Galloway, who selflessly gave of their time to help us gather new information and fact–check the updated history. Thanks, also, to Highland Park Middle School English teacher Yvonne Janik for her skillful editing.

We owe a debt of gratitude to Highland Park High School journalism teacher Elizabeth Perkins and her students (listed below) for their assistance in researching, writing, and envisioning the scope of this ambitious project.

Reagan Berry	Sarina Davila	Perri Demopulos
Rachel Drazner	Nathalie Elwood	Katie Harper
Hailey Humann	Caroline Jones	Morgan Kreston
Ashlyn Matthews	Macey McCarty	Libby Shelmire
Allison Smith	Maddi Thayer	Miranda Vernon
Eleanor Watson	Callaway Whitesell	

Our sincere thanks go to Highland Park Education Foundation Executive Director Jan Peterson, Alumni Association Director and 1990 graduate Jenni Scoggins, and Development Coordinator and 1964 graduate Beverly Vaughan, who shared their storehouse of knowledge and memorabilia with us. They contributed the sections of the book devoted to our alumni and the foundation and helped with research throughout this book.

We salute 1971 graduate Cindy Vaughan Kerr and 1979 graduate Debby Moore Baker, who generously volunteered as community liaisons for this book. They provided us with wise guidance and thorough fact–checking.

It is said that many hands lighten the load, and the extra help is especially appreciated on deadline. The volunteer dream team of Janet Carter, Wendy Crafton, and Cynthia Brogdon jumped in during the last few months before deadline and sorted through piles of scrapbooks and memorabilia items to find photos and more to bring 100 years of history to life. Thank you, ladies, for your countless hours of sorting, scanning, and all the fun you shared with us along the way!

We thank photographers Brad Bradley and Melissa Macatee for generously sharing their professional archives with us. These two talented journalists have shot pictures at more sporting events, pep rallies, and awards ceremonies than anyone can imagine! Aaron Cappotelli, Highland Park Middle School journalism teacher, shared a great many photos with us from his archives, and we also owe our sincere appreciation to Kim and David Leeson, who have photographed the first day of school and many other HPISD occasions for several years. Many of their memorable images are included in this book.

Hats off to several Highland Park High School interns for their contributions:
- 2014 graduate Mitchell Carr, who scanned countless photos
- 2012 graduate Vanisha Patel for finding photos to include in the history that was posted online in 2012
- 2013 graduate Molly Mannes, who put together a timeline that was posted online in 2012

Our sincere thanks go to HPISD Superintendent Dr. Dawson Orr and the HPISD School Board of Trustees (listed below) for their inspiration, support and counsel. They put us in touch with many people who took the time to tell us their stories.

School Board President Leslie Melson
School Board Vice President Jim Hitzelberger
School Board Finance Officer Joe Taylor
School Board Secretary Cynthia Beecherl
Trustee Kelly Walker
Trustee Paul Rowsey
Trustee Sam Dalton

Learning about the people and events that have shaped the last 100 years in HPISD has been a fascinating journey. We hope that you enjoy reading this historical account, compiled not only from the sources listed above, but also from the dozens of individuals who took the time to review this book before its publication. We also thank the many community members who dropped off photos and memorabilia to be used in Centennial displays and in this book. It has been an honor to work with every one of you!

The HPISD Communications Team

Helen Williams
David Hicks
Tammy Weingand
Jacki Moran
Elena Harding

Foreword

We count ourselves fortunate to be here during this historic marking of 100 years of Highland Park Independent School District. The words that are carved in stone above the entrance to Highland Park High School say it all:

Enter to Learn
Go Forth to Serve

Although the current high school did not open its doors until 1937, that same spirit of dedication to learning and service existed from the moment the very first campus — John S. Armstrong School — welcomed its students in 1914. Since then, the commitment to providing the children of this special place with an outstanding education has remained constant.

During its first 100 years, seven superintendents and 90 School Board members have led this district, and we are proud to carry on this mission today. The landscape may have changed, but the focus remains the same: serving our students in partnership with their parents and the larger community.

It has long been said that the schoolhouse is the heart of every community, and here in Highland Park ISD, it is our privilege and honor to be a part of something treasured by so many.

It is our hope that you enjoy exploring the history of our schools and the people who have made them the extraordinary places they are.

In gratitude and appreciation,

Dr. Dawson Orr
Superintendent of Schools

Mrs. Leslie Melson
School Board President

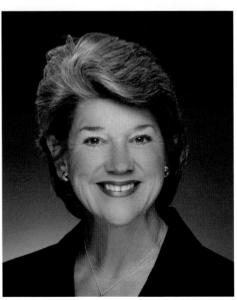

ENTER
TO LEARN

GO FORTH
TO SERVE

This is an altered photo illustrating the tradition of students entering at a young age to learn and leaving as graduates going forth to serve. This image was originally used as a cover photo for a School Board honors application.

Highland Park

Independent School District

1914   2014

Celebrating 100 years of excellence in learning and service

Students prepare for a night of trick–or–treating in the Park Cities in 1948.

History
of
Highland Park Schools

Oct. 12, 1914: The first day of school

An amazing journey began at John S. Armstrong School on Oct. 12, 1914. That was the day Highland Park ISD first opened its doors to 95 students. The tiny school, made up of only four rooms plus a basement, was led by Principal Belle Francis, who was known to ride her horse to school and hitch it to a post alongside the cream–colored brick building.

One hundred years later, Highland Park ISD serves more than 7,000 students on seven campuses. Today, the horse and hitching post are long gone. Yet remaining constant is the spirit of the community and its dedication to serving children.

Looking back over a century of excellence, one has to wonder what it is that makes this place unique. Highland Park alumni have gone on to make their mark in every imaginable field. The list includes a Nobel Prize laureate, Academy Award winners, Tony and Grammy Award winners, Pulitzer Prize recipients, Olympic gold medalists, Rhodes scholars, a two–time Cy Young Award winner, a Heisman Trophy winner, Hall of Fame athletes, an astronaut, law and business leaders, entrepreneurs, scientists, doctors, artists, mayors, a governor and valedictorians of West Point and the Naval Academy who graduated in the same year. No doubt, the legacy will continue for centuries to come.

HARPER & CO

Above: The Highlander *yearbook was originally produced by a group of students in the 1916–17 school year.*

Far left: *Mrs. Frank Mitchell Gray was the first PTA president at John S. Armstrong School.*

Left: *A photo from 1910 of the pecan tree that is still standing on Armstrong Parkway.*

This book is committed to capturing some of our proudest moments and tracing our history. To do so, we must look back before 1914, when the community's founding fathers first envisioned a place called Highland Park.

Before 1914: The little red schoolhouse

In 1906, John Scarborough Armstrong purchased 1,400 acres of prairie about five miles from downtown Dallas. Armstrong's sons–in–law, Edgar Flippen and Hugh Prather, became his business partners, and following Armstrong's death, they developed Highland Park, a place that lives up to its name. "Highland" refers to the fact that the neighborhood sits 100 feet higher than surrounding areas. "Park" reflects that 20 percent of the land is dedicated to parks, creeks and lakes.

In 1907, distinguished landscape architect and city planner Wilbur David Cook, who had just finished planning the community of Beverly Hills, Calif., joined the team. The first few blocks went on sale in 1908, and the first three houses were built on Lexington Avenue.

With families came children, and with children came the need for education. Perhaps no one exemplified this more than Michael Costello, father of eight, who built one of the first homes in Highland Park at the northeast corner of Lexington Avenue and Abbott Avenue. Costello and other early settlers, including H.J. Curtis, Hugh Prather and W.O. Connor, bought a frame house on McKinney Avenue to be used as a school. They moved it to what is now Abbott Park, and the little red schoolhouse opened in 1909 under the name "Highland Park School."

In November 1913, the Town of Highland Park was incorporated. The town built a fire station, and residents decided it was time to create their own school district.

1914–1919: A FACULTY OF FOUR

- Mary Innis, kindergarten teacher
- Katherine Mansfield, first–grade teacher
- Anne Rose McLean, second–grade teacher
- Principal Belle Francis, who taught a handful of students in grades 3–9

Top: A group of students and faculty members in front of the little red schoolhouse in 1911.

Above: Students celebrated May Day at John S. Armstrong School in 1915.

Right: John S. Armstrong purchased 1,400 acres of land, which his sons–in–law would develop into the Town of Highland Park.

1914–1919: Building a new school system

Wasting no time, community leaders presented a petition for the creation of Highland Park School Independent District on April 14, 1914, and the petition was granted on May 5 of the same year.

Highland Park ISD was born, and a Board of Trustees was selected to lead the new school system.

The next challenge was finding land for a building to replace the little red schoolhouse.

Mrs. Alice Armstrong, the widow of John S. Armstrong, donated the plot of land bounded by Cornell Avenue, Byron Avenue and St. John's Drive for the first school. She made the gift in honor of her late husband, and the school board thought it was only fitting that the district's first school should be named after Mr. Armstrong.

Top: HPISD students used the Dinkey trolley to get around town.

Far right: The Flippen–Prather Realty Co., founded by John S. Armstrong's sons-in-law, originally developed Highland Park.

Right: The first edition of The Highlander *yearbook from 1916–17.*

THE HIGHLANDER

1916   1917

Highland Park

The South's Finest Residence Section

Building Lots Average But $35.00 A Front Foot

FLIPPEN-PRATHER REALTY CO.

November 1913

Town of Highland Park incorporated

Petition granted to create Highland Park Independent School District

May 5, 1914

Mrs. Alice Armstrong, the widow of John S. Armstrong, donated the land for HPISD's first school. The School Board recognized her generosity by naming the school after her husband.

The school board authorized the construction of the district's first school, and it was completed in October 1914. The building featured cream–colored brick and consisted of four rooms, along with a basement that held another classroom and two large play areas for students to use during bad weather. There was no cafeteria, so students who lived nearby walked home for lunch. Others brought their lunches and ate at picnic tables and under the trees in the schoolyard.

Armstrong grows in numbers and support

Armstrong's parents wholeheartedly supported their new school, and Mrs. Frank M. Gray was named president of the school's first Parent Teacher Association. The organization adopted the slogan "For the welfare of the child" and boasted 44 members its first year.

By 1916, the young school's student enrollment had grown to 140 students in nine grades, and its faculty increased to 12 teachers. Belle Francis continued as principal, and the arts were added to the curriculum, reflecting a dedication to cultural enrichment that thrives today.

A special thanks to Mrs. Armstrong

In 1917, the first volume of *The Highlander* yearbook was published, and it was affectionately dedicated to Mrs. John S. Armstrong with the following words:

"TO HER who has ever proven in every way a faithful friend of our beloved school, and an ardent sympathizer in and promoter of its best interest, to Mrs. John S. Armstrong, this, our first volume is affectionately dedicated."

October 12, 1914

*First day of school at
John S. Armstrong School*

First volume of The Highlander
yearbook published

1917

SMU's Dallas Hall under construction in 1915.

CONSTRUCTION HIGHLIGHTS

- **July 16, 1914:** The newly formed school board approved $30,000 in bonds to build Armstrong School.
- **Summer of 1916:** Armstrong's second floor is completed, adding four classrooms, a clinic and an office.

WWI DONATIONS

During WWI, students raised money and collected supplies to donate to soldiers. Donations included:

- 14,400 gun wipes
- 90 washrags
- 49 face towels
- eight hospital pillows
- one refugee baby quilt
- one soldier's quilt
- 31 cootie bags, which soldiers put their clothes in to be boiled to remove "cooties"
- eight sweaters

SMU's long–standing relationship with HPISD

Alice Armstrong's generosity did not end with Armstrong School. She went on to donate 100 acres for the Southern Methodist University campus, the area where Gerald J. Ford Stadium now stands. William W. Caruth Sr. gave a half interest in an additional 725 acres.

SMU opened in 1915, to a great extent because of the efforts of its first president, Dr. Robert Stewart Hyer, the namesake of Hyer Elementary, which would be built more than three decades later.

Supporting the soldiers & community during WWI

During World War I, there was a shortage of fresh vegetables, so pupils planted and maintained war gardens on school property. The vegetables were distributed both to Armstrong families and to many in need. Students also organized War Saving Societies. A Junior Red Cross Society recorded the work done by the children in admiration of their willingness and ability to do their part. Under the leadership of President Mrs. C. E. Hudson, the Armstrong PTA raised money to send Christmas boxes with food, clothing and toys to orphans in France. Both the students and volunteers of Armstrong showed patriotism and compassion in their efforts to make a difference during wartime.

Highland Park ISD History (1920–1929)

The '20s were a time of tremendous change, both in Highland Park ISD and across the country. Middle–class Americans were buying Ford Model T cars, which soon lined the street in front of the high school. Thanks to passage of the 19th Amendment, women voted for the first time in 1920.

PTA begins its tradition of running campus cafeterias

Superintendent H.E. Gable, the PTA and the School Board met to identify the future needs of the district. In pointing out the larger needs of the school to the PTA, Gable listed a bigger lunchroom, a library, refrigeration of the drinking water and adequate physical training facilities. The School Board offered to equip a lunchroom if the PTA would manage and finance it. With earnings from rummage sales, candy sales and entertainment, the PTA raised the funds to put a lunchroom into operation at Armstrong School in January 1921. The lunchroom

Far left: Capt. R. G. Ghiselin helped institute the ROTC program at Highland Park High School.

Left: More houses began to pop up in the Park Cities, as shown in this 1922 photo of the corner of Hillcrest Avenue and University Blvd.

Above: A group of Armstrong students pose for a class photo in 1928.

was installed in the west end of the basement that formerly held the boys play area.

Thus, Armstrong PTA began the long–running tradition of PTAs running the cafeterias on every HPISD campus. To this day, parents, grandparents and other volunteers enjoy serving meals and visiting with one another, faculty members and, of course, the students who sometimes can't resist grabbing a quick hug before returning to class.

A decade of tremendous growth

Above: *An early photo of the HP football team in the mid–1920s.*

Left: *Alfred "Big 'Un" Rose played for the Scots football team from 1923 to 1925, and was named MVP of the University of Texas football team. He would go on to play eight seasons in the NFL, and won a championship with the Green Bay Packers in 1936. Rose is a member of the Texas High School Football Hall of Fame.*

The Town of Highland Park continued to boom, along with SMU. The City of University Park grew up around the university, incorporating in 1924. As word spread about the special community known as the Park Cities, HPISD grew by an average of 200 new students each year. This created a building boom, with three new campuses opening during this phenomenal decade: Highland Park High School in 1922, Bradfield Elementary in 1926 and University Park Elementary in 1928.

Before 1922, most Highland Park students who were of high school age had to ride the trolley down Cole Avenue to Dallas to attend Bryan Street High School, which no longer exists. Some attended the Morgan School, the Powell Training School on Binkley Avenue (which later became the site of Park Cities Kindergarten), Hockaday School for Girls (which was later the site of the Dallas YWCA Residence on Haskell), Ursuline Academy, St. Mary's Episcopal School for Girls (later part of St. Matthew's Cathedral on Ross), or the Terrill School for Boys on Swiss Avenue in order to complete their high school education.

CONSTRUCTION HIGHLIGHTS

- **1920:** HPISD purchased 11 lots, which became the district's first high school in 1922.

- **1922:** Highland Park High School opened on Normandy Avenue, where the current Highland Park Middle School sports field area is located. Superintendent Gable moved his office from Armstrong to HPHS.

- **1923:** A third, northern wing was added to Armstrong School. The new wing completed the "H" formation of the school and provided 12 new classrooms. That same year, a cafeteria was added in the basement of Armstrong's northern wing.

- **1925:** Bond election passed, authorizing $250,000 to construct two elementary schools. To conserve money, the same blueprints were used for both buildings — two–story brick structures with 12 rooms each.

- **1926:** Bradfield School, named after School Board President John S. Bradfield, opened. Located south of Mockingbird Lane and north of Southern Avenue, the school opened that fall after the end of the first six weeks grading period. The crowding was so severe at Armstrong that before Bradfield opened, there were often two teachers to a classroom and two students sharing a desk. When Bradfield opened, six teachers left Armstrong to teach at the new school.

- **1928:** University Park School opened with an enrollment of 165 students and six teachers, four of whom left Armstrong to staff the new school. A marker on the second floor commemorates the placement of a container with American and foreign coins, copies of Dallas newspapers and a Bible in the building's cornerstone. Nowhere does it mention a date when the items should be unearthed, so it is assumed they still remain there today.

Top: The original high school opened in 1922, and the building would later serve as the junior high and middle school.
Center: John S. Bradfield School opened in 1926.
Above: University Park School opened in 1928.

HP celebrates first graduates in 1924

Highland Park ISD held its first high school graduation ceremony on Monday, June 2, 1924. There were 34 graduates in total — 23 girls who wore white afternoon dresses and carried spring flowers and 11 boys who wore white flannel trousers and blue sport coats. Valedictorian Mary Margaret Taylor led the class in the ceremonies, which were held in the auditorium of the original high school campus on Normandy Avenue. The 34 graduates had grown up together and were among the first students to attend Armstrong School in 1914.

In the 1924 *Highlander*, the senior class proclaimed, "Many schools live merely on the momentum and traditions they have gathered in the more flourishing days of past. We are proud of our short past, but we are prouder of the Highland Park High School that is to be."

Alumni Association

In the 1928 *Highlander*, the early Alumni Association was mentioned as an organization open to "every student who receives a diploma from Highland Park High School." Formed in 1924, the meetings were held twice a year in December and June. By 1927, the association had 37 members. In the *Highlander*, the Alumni Association listed the latest information on graduates' schooling beyond high school, occupation and where they were living.

H.E. GABLE
HPISD'S FIRST SUPERINTENDENT

H. E. Gable became HPISD's first superintendent in 1920 and served the district until 1945. He came from Greenville, Texas, where he taught physics and headed the Academy Department of Besley College. He was known for closely working with parents and community leaders and for his calm style of leadership.

Far left: *A rendering of a Scot playing the bagpipes was one of the high school's early logos.*

Left: *These monthly report cards, from 1923–24 and 1924–25, were sent to parents.*

Above: *Students pose for a class photo in front of Armstrong School in 1929.*

1920	First lunchroom opened at Armstrong School	1922	First Highland Park High School football team formed	1923
H. E. Gable became HPISD's first superintendent	January 1921 — Highland Park High School opened on Normandy Avenue	1923		First Highland Park High School band formed

Mascot changes from coyote to Highlander

The first high school mascot was the coyote, and the team colors were orange and black. When Coach Floyd Betts arrived to coach the first Highland Park football team in 1923, he changed the mascot to the Highlander and the colors to blue and gold. In 1926, football games were led by the first squad of cheerleaders, with Artie Niendorff as head cheerleader and Mable Veal and Tom Nash rounding out the group. The small but mighty squad was praised in the yearbook as helping to lead the Highlanders to victory.

Band and ROTC programs form winning partnership

In the years before World War II, most Dallas high schools had strong Reserve Officer Training Corps (ROTC) programs. Highland Park started a volunteer unit in 1924, which became compulsory for boys in 1926. A month after becoming mandatory, the HPHS ROTC unit won the state competition. By 1928, it was the largest organization on campus, and the opening and closing of each school day was announced by an ROTC member playing a bugle, firing a cannon and raising or lowering the U.S. flag.

Under the direction of R.B. Ford and W.R. Ford, the first high school band was organized in 1923. Four years later the band became part of the ROTC and won first place as the best ROTC band in the state.

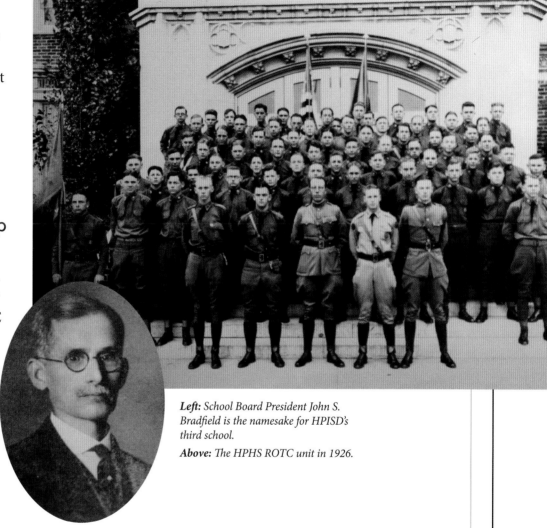

Left: School Board President John S. Bradfield is the namesake for HPISD's third school.
Above: The HPHS ROTC unit in 1926.

First high school graduation ceremony	1924	First Alumni Association formed	1924	John S. Bradfield School opened	1928
June 2, 1924	City of University Park incorporated	1924	First ROTC unit formed	1926	University Park School opened

HPISD continues its expansion

The 1930s were a difficult time for most Americans, as the Great Depression ravaged the country. Community members in the Park Cities also suffered hardship, but they continued to prove their commitment to education. Despite financial limitations, the district and the community worked to improve facilities to help handle the influx of students.

Reconfiguration of grade levels

Before the new high school opened, HPISD students in grades 1–7 attended elementary school, and students in grades 8–11 attended the high school. When the new high school opened on Emerson Avenue in 1937, the campus on Normandy Avenue became a junior high school. Twelfth grade was added, and the system changed: grades 1–6 attended elementary school, grades 7–9 attended junior high school, and grades 10–12 attended high school.

A tradition begins

In 1934, a new instrument appeared alongside the band and became an instant tradition: the bagpipe. The Dads Club paid for the new instruments used by the all–female piper crew, which played next to the band during halftime at football games. To this day, the rich, full tones from a bagpipe are a familiar sound to anyone who has attended an HP football game.

Before the tradition of wearing a cap and gown for graduation ceremony, HPHS girls wore white dresses, as seen here in 1934.

New publications appear at HPHS

During the 1930s, two new HPHS publications appeared and are still published today. The first editorial staff of *The Bagpipe*, HPHS's student–run newspaper, was formed in 1933. A student directory was published in 1939 and was called *The Clan*. It included 1,200 names and cost 10 cents to purchase.

CONSTRUCTION HIGHLIGHTS

- **1931:** A stage was added to Armstrong.

- **1932:** A new gym was added to Armstrong.

- **1937:** The new Highland Park High School, shown above, was built on Emerson Avenue, where it currently stands. The high school cost taxpayers approximately $400,000, and the campus was said to be one of the most modern and best–equipped high school buildings in the Southwest.

- **1937:** The old high school on Normandy Avenue was converted into Highland Park Junior High School.

Above: A group of students play the traditional HPHS bagpipes, accompanied by a drum, in 1934.

Right: The proud winners of the first Blanket Award are shown in 1938. The award is still given to seniors today.

Far right: Members of the first HPHS newspaper staff in 1933.

NEW HIGH SCHOOL FEATURES

The new high school on Emerson Avenue boasted:

- 32 classrooms
- two gyms
- two auditoriums
- a library
- a cafeteria
- an armory
- a clinic

- offices for student publications
- a public address system
- administration offices
- tennis courts
- a greenhouse
- a football field "with permanent seats for the comfort of the spectators"

The Kiltie
1 9 3 6

Principal Wiseman helps elevate high school's status

One of the most influential administrators in the history of the district was Ben Wiseman, who served as Highland Park High School's principal from 1928 to 1963. Wiseman is credited with setting and maintaining the high standards for which Highland Park is nationally known. He introduced advanced classes and diagnostic testing in math and English, hired the school's first counselor in 1934, initiated the student council, founded the Key Club and established a developmental reading program. Wiseman was posthumously honored at the inaugural Distinguished Alumni Awards ceremony in 1989 as the Distinguished Service Award winner. His name is still revered in the high school halls and across the community.

Top right: The 1935 Pep Squad helped cheer on the HP Scots.
Right: Ben Wiseman was a longtime HPHS principal, serving from 1928 to 1963.
Above: These students published the first edition of The Kiltie, *the high school's student handbook, in 1936.*

First Bagpipe *staff formed at HPHS*

1934

New Highland Park High School campus opened on Emerson, 12th grade added; old high school building converted into Highland Park Junior High School

1939

1933

Dads Club donated bagpipes to piper crew who played during halftime of football games

1937

First HPHS student directory, The Clan, *published*

Highland Park ISD History (1940–1949)

World War II began in late 1939 and lasted until 1945. After the attack on Pearl Harbor in 1941, more than 16 million Americans fought in the war, some of whom were HPISD fathers and alumni.

"I vividly remember my father driving off to leave for war," 1952 graduate Julie Ann O'Connell said. "It was scary not knowing if your daddy was going to come home again."

Scots help on the home front

During the war, HP students saved candy wrappers for tinfoil, mailed copies of *The Bagpipe* to Highland Park alums in the military overseas, took first-aid classes, helped the Red Cross and sold war bonds. In 1942–43 alone, more than 90 percent of the student body bought war bonds or stamps, totaling more than $70,000. In 1943, students started a memorial fund for alums who were killed in battle.

The war also had a direct effect on HPISD in the form of a steel shortage. Hyer Elementary School was originally scheduled to open in 1941, but the shortage pushed back the debut until 1949.

School Board president leads campaign for new YMCA building

In 1947, Dr. Shirley Hodges, a respected Dallas pediatrician, was elected to the School Board. He served through 1951, including a stint as president. He was also the health officer for the City of University Park, the original team doctor for the Highland Park Scots, president of the Southwest Amateur Athletic Union and founder of the Park Cities YMCA, which he created in 1944. Its first building was a home at 3802 University Blvd., right next to the University Park City Hall.

Top: *Doak Walker and Bobby Layne anchored the HPHS football team in the 1940s. They would both be inducted into the Pro Football Hall of Fame.*
Right: *An HPHS diploma from 1947.*
Below: *The first HPHS prom was held in 1947.*
Bottom: *A report card from the 1946–47 school year.*

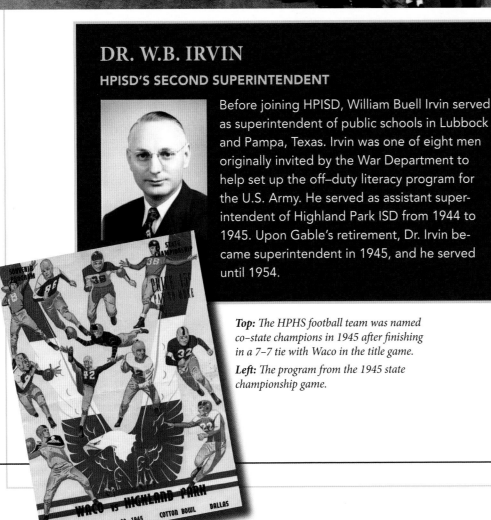

DR. W.B. IRVIN

HPISD'S SECOND SUPERINTENDENT

Before joining HPISD, William Buell Irvin served as superintendent of public schools in Lubbock and Pampa, Texas. Irvin was one of eight men originally invited by the War Department to help set up the off-duty literacy program for the U.S. Army. He served as assistant superintendent of Highland Park ISD from 1944 to 1945. Upon Gable's retirement, Dr. Irvin became superintendent in 1945, and he served until 1954.

Top: *The HPHS football team was named co-state champions in 1945 after finishing in a 7–7 tie with Waco in the title game.*

Left: *The program from the 1945 state championship game.*

Today, the gazebo at Goar Park stands at that exact spot. The creation of the YMCA had a major impact on the Park Cities, bringing recreational sports to young people.

Dr. Hodges soon led a campaign to build a new YMCA facility in the Park Cities. In 1946, Karl Hoblitzelle donated a city block, bounded by Preston Road, Normandy Avenue, Connerly Drive and Shenandoah Street — eight residential lots at a total value of $50,000 — to build a new YMCA. Residents were asked to donate $90 each, paid out over three years, and the funds were raised. The new building was completed in 1951, and the bittersweet part of the dedication was that Dr. Hodges, the facility's driving force, died of a heart attack at the age of 53 just before the building was completed. At the time, he was president of the HPISD Board of Trustees and had just been elected as the president of the North Texas Association of School Boards.

During its early years, the YMCA offered sports for young men only, and Dr. Hodges was the father of three daughters. People asked him why he was so dedicated to boys sports when he had no sons, and he smilingly replied, "I am trying to build men suitable to call on my daughters."

HPISD welcomes a new school to its family

The land for Hyer Elementary was purchased in the 1930s and included 7.5 acres bounded by Caruth Boulevard, Colgate Avenue, Pickwick Lane and a creek where Tu-

"Scottie Sweetheart" tradition began at HPHS, now known as Homecoming Queen

1945

1943

Dr. W. B. Irvin became HPISD's second superintendent

lane Boulevard is today. Noted architect Mark Lemmon designed the building, which cost $408,000 to construct.

Robert S. Hyer School opened Jan. 24, 1949, and was named in honor of the man who spearheaded the founding of Southern Methodist University. Hyer served as SMU President from 1911 to 1920.

On the first day of school at Hyer, students walked all the way from University Park Elementary to attend classes. More than 250 students lived in the Hyer attendance zone by the time it opened.

Newton Manning served as Hyer's first principal, and he was known for his larger–than–life personality. He had grown up in the area and had worked as a clerk at University Grocery on Hillcrest Avenue. He was popular with the students, especially when he brought goats, chickens and other animals to school for them to see. Manning was also known for turning on the school's intercom and breaking into a song right in the middle of class.

HP establishes itself as a sports champion

Highland Park High School sports, most notably football, enjoyed a great deal of success over the years, especially in the 1940s when the Scots' 10–year cumulative record was 105–21–2. The decade began with Redman Hume as the school's fifth head coach, who had a 45–26–1 record and was the winningest coach in HP history at the time.

The Doak Walker–Bobby Layne glory days of football started in the mid–1940s when Rusty Russell coached the Scots from

CONSTRUCTION HIGHLIGHTS

- **1949:** Hyer School opens, delayed by a steel shortage from WWII.

Top right: Newton Manning served as Hyer School's first principal.

Right: A program from the Highlander Music Festival in 1949. The Music Festival invited top bands, choruses and orchestras from all over the country, and even Canada.

Above: Robert S. Hyer, the namesake for Hyer School, also served as president of SMU from 1911 to 1920.

FOURTH ANNUAL HIGHLANDER Music Festival
BANDS · CHORUSES · ORCHESTRAS
APRIL 29-30, 1949
HIGHLAND PARK SCHOOLS, DALLAS, TEXAS

HPHS football team tied for state championship

1945

January 24, 1949

Robert S. Hyer School opened

Above: A Coca-Cola advertisement from a 1940s football program showed what referees' hand signals stood for.

Right: Three students pose with a Scottie dog mascot in 1947.

1942 to 1945, advancing the team to the state finals in 1944 and 1945. The 1943 team scored 455 points that season, setting a Scots record. The 1945 team battled Waco to a 7–7 tie for a co–state championship in front of a crowd of 45,700 at the Cotton Bowl. During their high school years, Layne and Walker also led their Highland Park basketball team to the state final four in 1943 and 1944.

In 1943, the football team nominated four finalists to be "Scottie Sweethearts." The practice continues as the Homecoming Queen tradition, with the winner determined by a vote by the student body.

After graduating, Walker and Layne went on to become All–Americans for the SMU Mustangs and Texas Longhorns, respectively. When Walker and Layne, who were friends but had polar opposite personalities and lifestyles, reunited in the NFL in the same Detroit Lions backfield, those Scots sparks began to fly again. Incredibly, the quarterback and running back from the same high school backfield led their pro team to two NFL championships in the 1950s, a phenomenon that sports followers still talk about today. Years later, both Layne (in 1967) and Walker (in 1986) were inducted into the Pro Football Hall of Fame. Layne held the Detroit Lions team record for passing yards from 1958 until 2013, when it was broken by fellow HP Scot Matthew Stafford, a 2006 graduate.

The brief reign of the Scottish Terrier mascot

In the early 1940s, fans began calling Highland Park the "Scotties," naming the Scottish Terrier as the mascot and painting a large Scottie dog on Highlander Stadium. Former players returning from the war discovered that their alma mater had "gone to the dogs," and a public meeting was called to discuss the situation. At that meeting, it was determined that the Scot Highlander would be the only symbol on the stadium.

Superintendent Gable retires

After 25 years as head of the Highland Park Independent School District, Superintendent Gable retired in 1945. Looking back at the development of the Park Cities schools during the quarter century, he said in his letter to the School Board that enrollment had grown from 433 to 4,621, and that school district property value had increased from $129,000 to $1,762,974.

Gable always held that character development was essential to shaping responsible citizens. He reiterated this notion by including this quote on every report card: "All agree that education for good citizenship should be the chief aim of schools. Training for citizenship is more a matter of developing the right spirit than of teaching facts."

Gable spoke of his quarter century of service: "If I had any part in helping to make better men and women out of these boys and girls, this is my greatest return."

He was given the well–deserved title of Superintendent Emeritus.

Highland Park ISD History (1950–1959)

Changes across the nation & in HPISD

In 1950, President Harry S. Truman, during his second term as president, led our nation as the Korean War began. After three years of fighting, a truce was signed between North and South Korea at the 38th parallel. In 1953, President Dwight D. Eisenhower was inaugurated as the 34th president and served two terms.

As the country experienced a change in leadership, so did the district. Dr. W.B. Irvin retired as district superintendent in 1954, and Frank Monroe took his place, continuing as superintendent until 1974.

In 1955, Rosa Parks was arrested in Montgomery, Ala., for refusing to give up her seat and move to the back of a bus. Subsequently, Rev. Martin Luther King Jr. led a bus boycott that year and set the American Civil Rights Movement in motion. In 1958, HPISD changed its "whites only" policy, although the first African–American student wouldn't attend school in the district until 1964.

In 1957, the Soviet Union launched the Sputnik satellite, the first man–made object to orbit the Earth. NASA was founded in 1958 and launched a project to take the first Americans into space. Class of 1945 graduate Elliot See Jr. was selected as a member of NASA's Astronaut Group 2, a collection of astronauts that included Neil Armstrong.

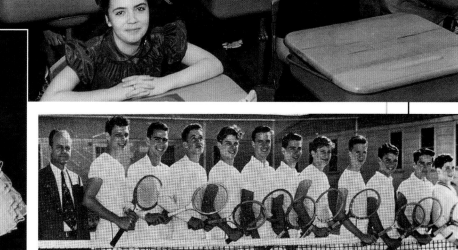

Top: *Armstrong students in the classroom in 1953.*

Above: *Coach Raymond Akin and the 1953 tennis team.*

Left: *The Highland Park Hillbillies perform at the Dallas Country Club in 1950.*

Center left: *Members of the ROTC escort their dates at the ROTC ball in 1955.*

CONSTRUCTION HIGHLIGHTS

- **Jan. 1950:** The School Board awarded a contract for additions to Armstrong.

- **Fall 1951:** The HPISD Administration Building opened at 7015 Westchester Dr.

- **1952–53:** Northeast and north-west additions were added to University Park Elementary. The cafeteria was enlarged in 1954, and a new kitchen was completed in 1956.

- **Sept. 1953:** Armstrong reopens after being rebuilt following the 1951 fire.

- **1955:** Trustees made plans to expand all six of the district's campuses, adding classrooms across the board. A library was also added to the junior high.

- **1958:** A second-floor annex was added to Armstrong, with an art/music room and four classrooms.

Top right: The original Armstrong School was destroyed by fire in 1951. The school was rebuilt in 1953.

Right: Batter up! The intramural girls softball team in 1955.

See was commander of the Gemini 9 mission but was tragically killed while flying a training jet in 1966 in St. Louis, Mo. He was posthumously named a Highland Park Distinguished Alumnus in 2010.

Fire destroys most of Armstrong

A fire devastated nearly all of Armstrong School on Nov. 26, 1951. According to *The Dallas Morning News*, Highland Park policeman Walter Paschall was on patrol when he drove by the school at 9:02 p.m. He radioed dispatcher John Crowley saying, "Flames are coming out of the roof. It looks like it's burning all over. Get all the fire trucks you can out here."

School Board members were meeting that evening at the Administration Building. They gathered, along with hundreds of others, around the burning building, according to the article.

Superintendent Irvin risked his life and ran into the burning building to rescue the only copies of the district's tax records, according to district history documents.

Fire destroyed most of Armstrong School	*1951*	*HPISD Administration Building opened on Westchester Drive*	*1953*
November 26, 1951	*Girls allowed to join band*	*1951*	*Armstrong campus reopened to students*

The fire destroyed two stories of the main building, but left the one–story annex intact. Mothers and teachers offered their homes for the school to use as classrooms.

Many classes were temporarily held at Highland Park Methodist Church.

In September 1953, Armstrong reopened its doors to students. According to *The Dallas Morning News*, the school cost approximately $700,000 to rebuild.

Superintendent Irvin, who was planning his retirement before the fire occurred, felt obligated to stay on with the district until the school was rebuilt. Armstrong repairs were completed in 1953, and a year later Irvin placed his request for retirement, which the School Board granted.

FRANK MONROE

HPISD'S THIRD SUPERINTENDENT

Frank Monroe moved from Midland, Texas, to become HPISD's third superintendent in 1954. His philosophy was that "schools must reflect the aspirations and desires of the people of the district," according to an article published in *The Dallas Morning News*, April 21, 1954. Monroe loved football and pep rallies and instituted a new tradition — the Victory Apple — that still continues. He retired in 1974 after 20 years of service.

Top: *HP Scots football team rushes the field after winning the 1957 state championship.*

Above: *The Scots celebrate after becoming state champs.*

Left: *Future Scot football stars played for the HP Junior High team.*

Frank Monroe became HPISD's third superintendent

1954

October 1955

Highland Park Junior High School awarded Freedom Medal

Lassie Bagpipers became part of HPHS band

1957

1957

HPHS graduates wore caps and gowns for graduation instead of traditional formal dress

In 1957, the senior class wore caps and gowns at graduation for the first time instead of the traditional formal dress that graduates had worn in previous years.

Left: *Superintendent Frank Monroe spurs on the high school at a pep rally.*

Below: *HPHS Drama students perform in the musical Rio Rita in 1957.*

Bottom: *Members of the 1957 Student Council helped lead the student body.*

Students make strides to keep up with the times

In 1951, girls were allowed to join the high school band for the first time. In 1957, the Lassie Bagpipers became part of the band. Previously, the Lassie Bagpipers were a pep squad known for a halftime performance called the Highland Fling.

The junior high was awarded the Freedom Medal in October 1955. Also called the George Washington Honor Medal of the National Freedom Foundation, it was awarded to organizations and institutions that exemplified responsible citizenship.

The National Merit Scholarship Corporation administered its first test in 1955, allowing students to compete for recognition and scholarships, and the highest achieving students were designated as National Merit Scholars. That year, after three rounds of testing, 10 Highland Park seniors were awarded certificates of merit.

Teacher compensation rises with number of students

As the number of students continued to grow in the district, so did the need for teachers. In 1951, the district hired 23 new teachers, bringing the total number to 240. As the decade continued, teachers asked for a pay raise as the number of students per teacher rose.

In 1954, the district increased its pay scale, and teachers with bachelor's degrees received $3,303 to $4,900 annually, compared with the old scale of $3,203 to $4,700, according to *The Dallas Morning News*.

ROTC RIFLEMEN HIT THE MARK

In May 1953, the high school's ROTC riflemen received American Legion marksmanship medals, the highest-ranking award for weapons qualification. Winners were chosen according to their records in matches during 1952–53.

Witnesses to a tragedy

The '60s were a time of change in both the district and the world. The decade began with the election of John Fitzgerald Kennedy as president.

The tragic assassination of President Kennedy on Nov. 22, 1963, was a defining moment in the country's history.

1950 HP graduate Pierce Allman, who was then program director for WFAA television and radio, was the first to report on the assassination from Dealey Plaza. He and a friend had decided to walk over from the newsroom to watch the motorcade. They found a spot on the corner across from the front door of the Texas School Book Depository. More than 50 years later, Allman described it as a moment that stands still in time.

"It's still so vivid. There's no sense of time at all," he said. "Sometimes, it's as if I'm seeing it in slow motion. I can see the whole thing. Even as I was processing it intellectually, part of me was saying, 'This is not happening. This is not real.'"

As soon as he realized what he had witnessed, he ran to find a phone to report on it immediately. On his way into the Book Depository, Allman encountered a thin young man with dark hair, a sallow complexion and circles under his eyes. Allman asked where he could find a phone. "In there," the man said, pointing with his thumb as he calmly left the building. Allman would later learn the man's name: Lee Harvey Oswald.

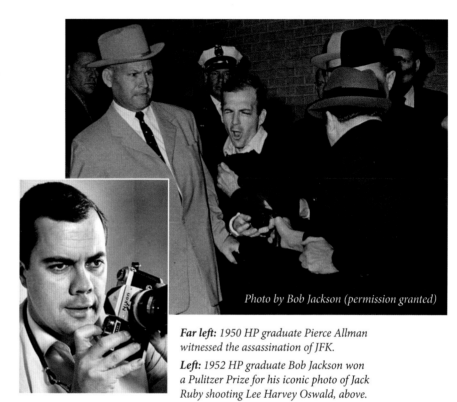

Photo by Bob Jackson (permission granted)

Far left: *1950 HP graduate Pierce Allman witnessed the assassination of JFK.*

Left: *1952 HP graduate Bob Jackson won a Pulitzer Prize for his iconic photo of Jack Ruby shooting Lee Harvey Oswald, above.*

1952 HP graduate and *Dallas Times Herald* photographer Bob Jackson was also at the scene that day.

"I was in the motorcade, and I saw a rifle in the window. I was one of four people who saw it. I was in the eighth car behind the president. So when the shots were fired and everything, we were facing the Book Depository, and I saw the rifle being drawn in. I had just tossed my film out to a reporter, so I was sitting there on the back seat of the convertible with an empty camera."

Jackson's camera was not empty two days later when suspected

50TH ANNIVERSARY
(source: *Living Tradition: The First 50 Years*)

- **Elementary enrollment:** 2,257 students, 134 teachers
- All teachers were college graduates, 40 percent had master's degrees
- Homeroom classes averaged 24 students each
- **HPJHS enrollment:** 1,327 students, 73 teachers
- 97 percent of teachers held college majors in the subjects they taught
- Three full–time counselors for students in grades 7–9
- The campus had 59 classrooms, five science labs, two art studios, two gyms, three music rooms, shops for wood and metal work and a speech studio
- **HPHS enrollment:** 1,363 students and 83 teachers
- Counseling staff expanded to five full–time positions
- Pupil–teacher ratio of 16.4:1
- Band marched 60 boys and 14 Highland Lassies
- Spring production of *Brigadoon* produced by a cast of 100 and an orchestra of 50
- Building had 59 classrooms

Above: Middle school students practice the French horn in 1968.
Far right: Armstrong students celebrate Thanksgiving in 1965.
Middle right: A high school student participates in a PE exercise in 1962.
Right: A young Armstrong student practices her penmanship in 1962.

Two HPHS graduates, Charles Otstott and Alton Thompson, graduated first in their respective classes at the U.S. Military Academy at West Point and the U.S. Naval Academy

1961

1960

End of two–class graduating system

assassin Lee Harvey Oswald was shot by nightclub owner Jack Ruby on the way to the courthouse. He captured the moment on film and was awarded the Pulitzer Prize for his photo.

"I was looking through my camera when I was aware that someone was stepping out to my right, and it was very quick. He took two steps and fired, and I fired (my camera) at the right time, apparently," he said.

"It was almost 2 p.m. before I was able to get back to the paper. I went into the darkroom and ran my film, and I remember looking at the wet film against the light, and it looked good. We made a quick, wet print and carried it out to the newsroom, and we realized what we had."

The photo remains one of the iconic images of the century, and the camera Jackson used is on display in the Sixth Floor Museum. Allman provides the audio tour narration for the museum, which hosts approximately 315,000 visitors a year.

Top right: Cheerleaders strike a pose in 1963.

Center: 1945 HP graduate and astronaut Elliot See, Jr. returns to speak at his alma mater.

Right: Football players receive the traditional victory apple during a 1964 pep rally.

Plane crashed into Bradfield School

September 27, 1967

Left: Alton Thompson, Class of 1956, and Charles Otstott, Class of 1955, both graduated as valedictorians of their military classes at Annapolis and West Point, respectively.

HP grads make service academy history

In 1960, President Eisenhower honored two district alumni: Charles Otstott (Class of '55) and Alton Thompson (Class of '56). They had been their respective class presidents at HPHS, were both winners of the prestigious Blanket Award, and both graduated first in their military academy class.

Otstott attended SMU for one year before attending West Point. Upon graduating from West Point, he was so decorated that it was said he "walked off with everything short of the Kissing Rock." Otstott went on to serve in the Vietnam War and was awarded the Bronze Star Medal and Silver Star Medal.

Thompson commanded his 3,600-man brigade at the Naval Academy, where he also captained the football team. He served as commanding officer of the nation's first Trident-class nuclear submarine, the *USS Ohio*, and as commanding officer of the nuclear attack submarine, the *USS Puffer*. He retired as a naval captain in 1984.

Time's 1960 accounting of these impressive accomplishments included an overview of Otstott's and Thompson's high school: "Highland Park High School, which serves two upper-class Dallas suburbs, University Park and Highland Park, is one of the toughest high schools academically in the Southwest. From 1957 to 1959, only 40 of its 1,022 graduates did not attend college. In 1960, the national ratio of graduating seniors to National Merit scholars was 1,666-to-1; at Highland Park, the ratio proved to be 183-to-1."

Changes big and small

The Vietnam War and changes in music, fashion and entertainment impacted the nation's culture and the district in many ways. Student interest in everything from current events to volunteerism sparked the formation of many new clubs and organizations.

At Highland Park High School, there had always been two graduating classes each year, one in January and one in June. The 1961 graduation marked the end of the two-graduating-class system, which had been in place since 1918.

Another landmark change was the 1963 retirement of longtime HPHS Principal Ben Wiseman, who dedicated 35 years of his life to upholding the standard of excellence for his school family.

Plane crashes into Bradfield Elementary

Sept. 27, 1967, was just like any other Wednesday, with students dismissed early at 3:10 p.m. so teachers could attend the weekly staff meeting. Many of the students were on the YMCA football team, which was practicing on the field. The peaceful routine was shattered at 3:40 p.m. when a small twin-engine plane crashed into Bradfield Elementary. The plane's left wing broke in half, sending the plane into the ground. It hit a car on Mockingbird Lane in its descent, slid through the bicycle racks, then crashed into the north wall of the school.

CONSTRUCTION HIGHLIGHTS

- **1961:** A new science wing was built at the high school.

- **1964:** New floors were installed in 49 new classrooms, and 1,400 movable desks were added to both the high school and junior high. Also in the high school, a 30–seat language laboratory was added to help in the study of French and Spanish. The auditorium was modernized, and new seats were added.

- **1964–1968:** Bond issues to finance renovations at all four elementary schools and construction at Highland Park High School, including:

  A field house, swimming pool and new basketball gym were added to the high school. The new basketball gym provided space for 1,600 spectators. Two hundred of the seats were padded seats for season ticket holders. The new 75x42–foot pool added in 1966 was designed not only for the swim team but also for physical education classes.

  Improvements were also made to the cafeteria, Highlander Stadium, and administrative and custodial offices.

  Construction began on two new wings, adding 22 new classrooms, a library and a planetarium. Carpeting and air conditioning were added. The cafeteria was updated, and computers were introduced to make schedules.

Tad Heimburger (Class of '74) will never forget seeing the plane heading straight for him as he was tying his books and clothes onto the back of his bike on the way to football practice.

"I was the only kid at the bike rack. When I looked up — this was very loud — I was seeing a plane spinning, and it was practically right on top of me. I watched it for long enough to see it do almost one rotation. I remember thinking that he was doing stunts," he said. "I thought, 'he's going to hit the trees or the telephone lines above me,' and I turned and ran inside the building. I had on football pants, and it had burned the backs of my leg, and the back of my neck and my hair was singed."

All seven people in the plane died on impact. Had it not been an early–dismissal day, the results might have been more tragic.

The Dallas Morning News gave the following details in a front–page story on Sept. 28, 1967:

"A witness, C.W. Culwell, was with one of the teams when he heard the plane coming in low.

Culwell, owner of a men's clothing store and himself a private pilot, said he looked up when he heard the plane and saw it heading down at a 45–degree angle.

The left wing was folded back against the fuselage, Culwell said . . . and it was obvious the airplane was totally out of control.

When the plane exploded, he said, 'There was no way we could get up close to help. What we ought to say our prayers about is that if it had hit 20 minutes earlier, there's no telling how many of our kids it would have killed.'"

Miraculously, no students were seriously injured when an airplane crashed only feet from Bradfield School on a school day in 1967.

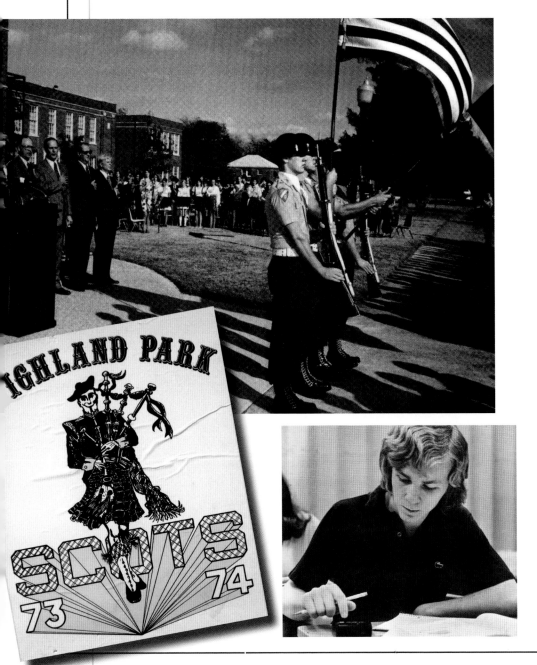

Progress marches alongside conflict

The '70s were a decade of contrast and conflict. In reaction to the continued U.S involvement in the Vietnam War, a wave of protests swept the country.

Technological advances made pocket calculators, VCR players, microwaves and cassette or eight–track tapes part of daily life. The computer industry was on the rise after the world's first microprocessor, the Intel 4004, was introduced, and personal computers were sold around the world. All of these developments influenced lifestyles immensely, especially those of students in the latter half of the decade. New technology began to spread into the schools, greatly affecting the process of education. HPHS acquired 10 new electronic calculators, which were referred to as "mini–computers," to replace slide rules in physics classes. Also, *The Clan* (the high school's student directory) was converted to computer sheets, which made it possible to be printed earlier and kept more up–to–date. Students gained easier access to information and tools, and teachers had new, exciting ways to present the information.

Robin Rees–Jones, '71, co-editor of *The Bagpipe*, reflected on the paradoxical nature of human progress, writing, "Man [had] learned to build a machine complex enough to travel to the moon, yet man still [could not] understand the most complex machine of all — man himself. Man cannot live on the moon, yet man [could not] live peacefully on earth."

Top: A dedication ceremony was held in 1974 to rename the Highland Park Middle School to Arch H. McCulloch Middle School. McCulloch served on the HPISD board for 22 years, making him the longest serving trustee to date.

Left: A high school student uses his pocket calculator in 1974.

Far left: The original Scot mascot from the 1920s was still being used in the 1970s.

ROTC

Although there was a dramatically increasing student population, the ROTC was rapidly losing members since the program became voluntary in 1963. This plan was initially enacted as a means to better the unit but eventually played a role in its downfall. Because of low membership and increasing necessity of resources for other programs, ROTC was disbanded in 1978.

Title IX spells out requirement for gender equity

In 1972, Title IX was passed requiring "gender equity for boys and girls in every educational program that receives federal funding."

The law applies to many areas of education, but it is perhaps best known for the changes it made to athletic programs. Before Title IX, only one in 27 female high school students participated in school athletics. After the law was passed, HPHS allowed girls to enroll and participate in many other activities previously restricted to boys, such as woodshop and ROTC, and made plans to expand and add girls locker rooms and a gym in upcoming construction projects.

As dress codes changed, girls were allowed to wear pants to school, as shown here in 1974.

CONSTRUCTION HIGHLIGHTS

- Work continued on construction funded by the 1968 bond issue, including the installation of air conditioning in all HPISD campuses.

- Construction continued on additions to HPHS:
  – a student commons where the east courtyard had been
  – an elevator for the handicapped
  – additional parking spaces
  – a new physical education facility adjacent to the boys gym that included basketball, volleyball, gymnastics and weight training facilities
  – an all–sports facility that replaced the health and safety education rooms
  – renovations to the pool area, including the installation of a diving board, a new ceiling and windows
  – additional classroom space to accommo–date the ninth grade, which had previ–ously been part of the junior high
  – a new library and a new planetarium

An addition to the high school was constructed in 1970.

HPISD named in desegregation lawsuit

Among the changes occurring in the '70s was desegregation. It proved to be a struggle because the only way to desegregate schools was to incorporate busing to change the racial makeup of individual schools within each district. HPISD and six other districts were named in a lawsuit for not achieving a proportional percentage of all races that matched that of the City of Dallas and Dallas Independent School District. HPISD's request to be dropped from the lawsuit was denied. One issue was that the only way for HPISD to change its racial proportion was to bus students across district lines. Even if HPISD changed attendance zones within the district, it would not affect racial makeup.

FIGHTING SCOT EMBLEM

On Nov. 18, 1977, the popular Fighting Scot emblem was created and published on the front cover of the program for the Highland Park vs. R.L. Turner football playoff game at Texas Stadium.

It was designed by nationally renowned sports and political cartoonist Bill McClanahan, a 1927 graduate of HPHS. McClanahan was a staff cartoonist at *The Dallas Morning News* for many years, and variations of his drawing of the fighting Scot are now used by many athletic teams at Highland Park.

Bill McClanahan

Top: *Girls wore their traditional PE uniform in 1974.*

Above: *UP fifth-graders take a class photo with their teacher in 1979.*

1970	Title IX passed, requiring gender equity in educational programs		1974	Dr. Winston C. Power, Jr. became HPISD's fourth superintendent
Freshmen became part of HPHS student body; junior high name changed to Highland Park Middle School		1972	Highland Park Middle School renamed Arch H. McCulloch Middle School	1974

According to Highland Park's attorney Dick Gray, HPISD did not currently permit inter–district transfers "and did not permit them at the time of the plaintiff's second amended complaint . . . nor did it permit them for years prior to them." Gray also pointed out that since the late '50s, the district had a policy "of accepting all students that live within [district lines] without regard to the race, creed, color, or national origin of such students," and that the policy had been strictly followed ever since. When Gray submitted a breakdown of HP's school enrollment since the '60s, it was clear that the minority enrollment in each school had barely exceeded 2 percent of the total enrollment, and that number matched that of its community. Finally, after five years, Highland Park became the last district to be dropped from the lawsuit in 1975.

DR. WINSTON C. POWER, JR.
HPISD'S FOURTH SUPERINTENDENT

Dr. Winston Power worked at Dallas ISD before joining HPISD as an administrative intern in January 1966. He served as assistant principal at Highland Park Junior High, as principal at University Park Elementary and as an elementary/secondary consultant before being named the fourth superintendent in Highland Park ISD's history. He served as superintendent from 1974 to 1990.

HPISD grew under Dr. Power's watch, as voters approved two bond issues that allowed renovations and additions to all of the district's campuses, in addition to the construction of Highlander Stadium in 1980, which is still used today for athletic competitions in grades 7–12.

"Dr. Power was a remarkable man and a very effective leader," said Becky Nugent, former HPISD Director of Communications. "He was a visionary with high expectations, and he also knew there was always room for improvement."

The HPISD Alumni Association honored Dr. Power with the Distinguished Service Award in 1994.

Right: *The Hyer PTA produced a cookbook in 1973.*

Left: *Armstrong students are cheered on by their parents during the 1977 field day.*

November 18, 1977

Fighting Scot emblem created

Class of 1934 grad Bill Clements was elected governor of Texas

1978

1978

ROTC program disbanded

Reconfiguration of grades occurs throughout the system

When the 1970 school year started at Highland Park High School, freshmen were part of the student body for the first time since 1936. The junior high changed its name to Highland Park Middle School, and the sixth grade was moved to the school from the four elementary schools.

Three years later the school board voted to change the name of the junior high to McCulloch Middle School, in honor of the late Arch H. McCulloch, the longest-serving trustee in HPISD history (1950–1972).

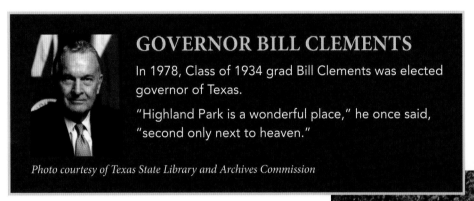

GOVERNOR BILL CLEMENTS

In 1978, Class of 1934 grad Bill Clements was elected governor of Texas.

"Highland Park is a wonderful place," he once said, "second only next to heaven."

Photo courtesy of Texas State Library and Archives Commission

Top right: *Students boogie down at the HPHS Beginnings Dance, following the first football game in 1977.*

Right: *The 1977 HPHS cheerleaders were always ready to support their Scots.*

Dress code gives students more options

The dress code began changing drastically for the first time in decades. Girls had been required to wear skirts or dresses. Culottes, which were shorts cut to look like skirts, were first permitted during the 1969–70 school year. In 1971, girls were allowed to wear pantsuits, and they were allowed to wear long pants in 1975.

Boys' hair was allowed to hang below the top of the dress shirt collar in 1975. In 1977, socks and belts became optional, and overalls were permitted if worn over a shirt.

Above: Dawn Lallier and Eddie Coker won first place in the 1977 talent show.

Below: Bob Jordan, shown here in 1978, was a beloved band director at HPHS.

Left: A group photo of a first-grade class at Bradfield during the 1978–79 school year.

Celebrating a new stadium in style

In 1980, Highlander Stadium opened its gates to a crowd that was ready for a true home game. The Scots had been playing at SMU's Ownby Stadium while the new stadium was being built.

Before the game began, a man parachuted in and delivered the game ball to Gov. Bill Clements, a proud graduate of the Class of 1934.

"It was a really exciting event with a lot of built–up anticipation," said Jeff Berry, a 1981 graduate. "Our motto, Scots Got Pride, was never more evident, and the opening fanfare was equally over the top. We crushed our opponents that night."

HP graduate awarded Nobel Prize in Physics

The year 1980 was also notable for the Scots in the field of science, when it was announced that 1948 graduate Dr. James Cronin and his fellow researcher Val Fitch won the Nobel Prize in Physics. They were lauded "for the discovery of violations of fundamental symmetry principles in the decay of neutral K–mesons," according to the Nobel Foundation.

That research led to the theory that the universe was formed by a "big bang" explosion billions of years ago.

Asked to translate his research into layman's terms, Dr. Cronin said, "It's highly technical, and it deals with quantum mechanics and particle physics. Interpreted in the broadest way, it allows us to understand why we live in a matter–dominated universe."

Cronin said it was gratifying to see how his discovery created a spark.

Top: *The new Highlander Stadium was built in 1980. It is still used today for various HPISD athletic events and activities.*

Above: *To celebrate the opening of the new stadium, a man parachuted into Highlander Stadium to deliver the game ball to Gov. Bill Clements.*

Far left: *Dr. James Cronin, Class of 1948, won the Nobel Prize in Physics in 1980.*

CONSTRUCTION HIGHLIGHTS

- **1980:** The new Highlander Stadium opens
- **1983:** Indoor Seay Tennis Center opens, thanks to a generous gift from Charlie and Sadie Seay
- **1988:** HPHS science wing is completed, including 10 classrooms and eight labs; renovations included journalism, business, typing, math, homemaking and photography classrooms

"It inspired a huge amount of research. I followed it up by doing additional experiments for about 10 more years, and then I moved into astrophysics and subjects concerned with cosmic radiation."

Cronin traces his interest in science to his days at HPHS and in particular to his physics teacher Charles H. Marshall.

"He was a superb teacher. He made us build things and do real experiments, as opposed to just working problems in a book," Cronin remembers.

As a Nobel Laureate, Cronin joined the ranks of the top scholars in the world, including Albert Einstein, who was awarded the Nobel Prize in 1921.

Top left: UP students in 1987 wave to the camera.

Right: The Seay Tennis Center was named after 1932 graduate Charlie Seay.

Far right: The captains of the 1988 Scots football team.

Dramatic changes in classroom, playing field

Even as people around the world scratched their heads trying to understand Cronin's findings on matter and antimatter, the landscape of public education in Texas was undergoing its own transformation. The 1984 passage of House Bill 72 introduced dramatic reforms to the state's system. The No Pass No Play rule stipulated that all students in extracurricular activities must have passing grades in order to continue participating. This affected students in all UIL competitions — athletics, the fine arts and academics.

The new law also required students to pass exit–level exams in order to graduate and put more stringent teacher certification requirements in place.

Students and teachers adjusted to the new system, and Highland Park ISD continued to grow, most dramatically in the area of activities for girls.

"To be a female athlete in any sport at Highland Park means you earn respect," said Jerry Sutterfield, who joined HPISD in 1985 as a metal shop and wood shop teacher. Sutterfield went on to coach boys and girls track and cross country, and he became the district's first Director of Women's Sports in 2003.

"Being strong, being outspoken and achieving high academic levels are the hallmarks of a female athlete at our school," he said. "Our girls want to succeed, whether it's on the field, in the gym or in the Academic Decathlon."

The Highland Belles made their debut in 1983, and continue to proudly wear their iconic fringe.

The Belles ring in a new era

The Highland Belles drill team began in 1983, and from the start, the organization was about hard work, discipline and character, in addition to excellent dancing.

Cathy Wheat, the founding director who went on to lead the team for 22 years, said the very first Belles came in with high expectations and a willingness to do what it takes to build a new program.

"These girls could unflinchingly devote themselves to the hard work ahead, wholeheartedly submit themselves to the hard work and discipline necessary to create a successful drill team, and willingly act as role models for girls throughout the school," she said.

With the team selected, the next big decision was the uniform. The girls considered the usual boots, cowboy hats and sequins, but they wanted something unique, so Wheat collaborated with art students. The result was a blue uniform with a yellow "V" symbolizing victory, white fringe and white Keds with high socks. More than three decades later, the uniform, fondly known as "the fringe," is still worn today.

New Highlander Stadium opened

1983

1980

Highland Belles
drill team began

HP SWIMMERS BRING HOME SIX OLYMPIC MEDALS

Three outstanding HP graduates made their mark in swimming in three consecutive Olympic competitions. Back home, Scots fans cheered on their hometown athletes during the 1984 Olympics in Los Angeles, the 1988 Olympics in Seoul and the 1992 Olympics in Barcelona.

THE WINNERS ARE:

- **Bruce Hayes, 1981 graduate:** gold medal, men's 4x200–meter freestyle relay (1984 Olympics)

- **Mike Heath, 1982 graduate:** gold medal, men's 4x100–meter freestyle relay; gold medal, men's 4x200–meter freestyle relay; gold medal, 4x100–meter medley relay; silver medal, individual 200–meter freestyle event (1984 Olympics)

- **Shaun Jordan, 1986 graduate:** gold medal, men's 4x100–meter freestyle relay (1988 Olympics); gold medal, men's 4x100–meter freestyle relay (1992 Olympics)

As a note, while these three Olympians earned their medals within just a few years of one another, 1948 graduate Skippy Browning is also a gold medal winner. He earned his gold medal in springboard diving in Helsinki in 1952.

The 1984 Olympic gold–medal–winning 4x200 freestyle relay team celebrates at the top of the podium. Two of the team members, Mike Heath, second from left, and Bruce Hayes, far right, are HPHS graduates.

The Belles celebrated their 30th anniversary in 2013 with the screening of a 30–minute documentary film "Beyond the Fringe." There were three shows on Dec. 17 at Highland Park Village Theatre, and the place was packed with Belles alumnae, friends and family, a testament to the lifelong effect that being on the iconic drill team has had on many of its members.

A precursor to Robin Hood

In May 1984, in the landmark case of Edgewood ISD vs. Kirby, the Mexican American Legal Defense and Educational Fund challenged the state's methods for funding public schools.

"The plaintiffs in the Edgewood case contested the state's reliance

Indoor Seay Tennis
Center opened

1984

1983

Highland Park Education
Foundation incorporated

on local property taxes to finance its system of public education, contending that this method was intrinsically unequal because property values varied greatly from district to district, thus creating an imbalance in funds available to educate students on an equal basis throughout the state," according to the Texas State Historical Association.

The case wound its way through the court system, and in October 1989, the Texas Supreme Court unanimously ruled in the plaintiffs' favor. The court ordered the legislature to put an equitable school funding system in place by the 1990–91 school year.

While "Robin Hood" had not yet become a household phrase, leaders in Highland Park closely followed the case and understood that big changes were in store for the district and the community in the years to come.

Education Foundation opens

It was clear that the court battle over school finance was far from over, and that a public–private partnership was the wisest strategy for preserving the tradition of educational excellence in HPISD. So community leaders organized the Highland Park Education Foundation, which incorporated as a nonprofit in 1984. For the first 10 years, foundation projects were volunteer–driven, and annual distributions were directed to student scholarships with occasional special gifts, such as seed funding, to start the HPHS Alumni Association.

As the years went on, the Foundation grew from a small operation to a fundraising powerhouse that partnered with PTAs, La Fiesta de las Seis Banderas, individual leaders and other community groups to help fund faculty salaries, teacher grants, teacher training and technology. Foundation fundraising efforts have grown steadily, thanks to the annual Mad for Plaid campaign. Gifts increased from $17,000 in 1993–94 to more than $2.5 million in recent years.

Top: The McCulloch Middle School cheerleading squad in 1987.
Above: *A group of Hyer students take a quick break from their field day activities in 1984.*

Highland Park ISD History (1990–1999)

HPHS revives Alumni Association

In 1990, HPHS revived its Alumni Association to provide an organization that would allow graduates to keep in touch and strengthen their connection to the district. Art Barnes, 1951 graduate, served as the first chairman in 1991.

Over the years, the association has built an alumni directory, planned numerous reunions and established scholarships for graduating seniors.

In addition to class reunions, there are two large celebrations every year: the Distinguished Alumni Awards and the Golden Scots Reunion.

The first Distinguished Alumni Awards program was held in 1989 and helped build the excitement for the re-establishment of the Alumni Association in 1990. In addition to the Distinguished Alumni Awards, which are given to three graduates every year, the association also gives a Distinguished Service Award to a former employee for outstanding service and the Highlander Award, which is given to an individual who has made a major contribution to HPISD. *For a list of honorees, see the Alumni section of this book.*

The Golden Scots Reunion began in 1994 to honor alumni who graduated at least 50 years earlier. With between 500 and 700 attendees, it is the largest gathering of alumni every year.

Top: The HPISD Alumni Association was re-established in 1990 with the help of these dedicated Scots.

Above: A student takes a swing during the 1990 Armstrong carnival.

Left: Former President George W. Bush was the keynote speaker during the 1990 HPHS Commencement Ceremony.

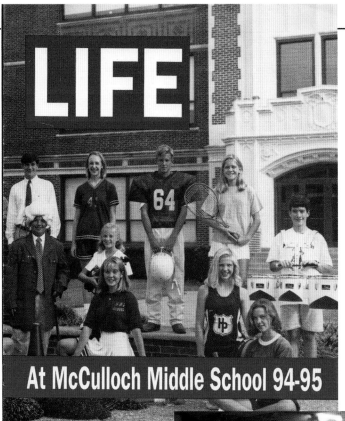

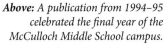

Robin Hood: Recapture of local tax dollars presents growing challenge

The '90s marked the enactment of Robin Hood, the state's practice of recapturing local tax dollars and redistributing them to districts across Texas. This was the legislature's solution to the Texas Supreme Court's 1989 order to put an equitable school funding system into place. Under Robin Hood, Texas recaptured property tax revenues from property-wealthy school districts and distributed those dollars to property-poor districts. Because of its valuable local tax base, Highland Park ISD was hit hard, with recapture payments hovering around 70 percent for many years. For example, in 2013–14, HPISD's recapture rate was 68 percent, requiring the district to send $69.3 million to the state. From 1991 to 2014, Highland Park ISD taxpayers paid a grand total of more than $1 billion to the state in recaptured dollars.

Above: A publication from 1994–95 celebrated the final year of the McCulloch Middle School campus.

Right: Eighth graders celebrate their last days in middle school with an end-of-year breakfast.

Far right: UP students successfully navigate a safety course during the 1990 Bike Rodeo.

1990

Dr. John P. Connolly became HPISD's fifth superintendent

1994

HPHS Alumni Association revived

1990

Golden Scots reunions began

The so-called Robin Hood system is now a household phrase, and district and community leaders took a two-pronged approach of raising money locally while trying to work with state leaders to mitigate the dramatic effect of so many tax dollars leaving the district. The reliance on private funding grew, and the Education Foundation, HPISD PTAs, Dads Clubs, Sports Club, Booster Clubs, La Fiesta de las Seis Banderas, HP Arts and other community supporters stepped up to raise the millions needed to fill the gap.

DR. JOHN P. CONNOLLY

HPISD'S FIFTH SUPERINTENDENT

In 1990, the School Board hired Dr. John P. Connolly as its fifth superintendent. Dr. Connolly came to Highland Park from Chappaqua Central School District in New York, where he had served as Superintendent of Schools.

Dr. Connolly assumed leadership of HPISD during a challenging time. He addressed the issues of rapid enrollment growth and the loss of local control that resulted from Robin Hood legislation. Dr. Connolly helped found the Texas School Coalition, an organization made up of more than 100 school districts that advocates for meaningful discretion of local boards over their district funds. He served as the group's first full-time executive director. Dr. Connolly served as HPISD superintendent from 1990 to 2001.

In 2012, he was awarded the Distinguished Service Award for his years of service.

Top: Armstrong students practice their keyboarding skills on Apple computers.

Above: Armstrong Principal Dr. Kenneth Thomas leads his campus in a parade during Spirit Day.

Left: A Bradfield student shows off his hula-hoop skills during the 1991 campus carnival.

Far left: The 1991 HPHS Commencement Ceremony at SMU's Moody Coliseum.

1995

New campus opened with two schools housed in one building – McCulloch Intermediate School and Highland Park Middle School

Highland Park Literary Festival began

1995

Literary Festival

The first Highland Park Literary Festival was held in 1995 as a collaboration between interested parents and the HPHS English Department. Now an annual event, the festival features more than 100 workshops conducted by accomplished journalists, novelists, songwriters, poets and playwrights. There is a student–run open–mic night, where students read their own work and an evening featuring a keynote speaker is open to the community. The Literary Festival is supported by La Fiesta de las Seis Banderas, HP Arts, the Highland Park High School PTA and individual donors.

LITERARY FESTIVAL KEYNOTE SPEAKERS

- Carol Higgins Clark, 1996–97
- Doug Wright, HP grad and Tony Award–winning playwright, 1997–98
- James Kelman, 1998–99
- Marion Winik, 1999–2000
- Don Graham, 2000–01
- Tim O'Brien, 2001–02
- George Plimpton, 2002–03
- Russell Banks, 2003–04
- Michael Chabon, 2004–05
- Kaye Gibbons, 2005–06
- Anchee Min, 2006–07
- Scott Simon, 2007–08
- Billy Collins, 2008–09
- Tobias Wolff, 2009–10
- Doug Wright, 2010–11
- Naomi Shihab Nye, 2011–12
- Markus Zusak, 2012–13
- Mark Salzman, 2013–14

Top right: *Bestselling author Markus Zusak signs autographs during the 2013 HP Literary Festival.*

Bottom right: *Bradfield students show off their prize pumpkin during fall activities in 1992.*

Top: Hyer football players, princesses, superheroes and more show off their 1999 Halloween costumes.

Above: Friends talk after class at Highland Park Middle School in 1997.

Left: MIS fifth–graders practice their pyramid skills in 1997.

Voters turn down 1998 bond issue but pass smaller version in 1999

With enrollment still increasing, HPISD proposed a $76 million bond package in 1998, which was not approved by voters. The most contentious issue surrounding the bond issue was the proposal for the construction of a fifth elementary school.

Voters approved a smaller bond issue of $49.95 million the following year to fund district-wide renovations, new technology systems, and equipment and additions to HPHS.

CONSTRUCTION HIGHLIGHTS

Early in the decade, the baseball field at the high school underwent construction. In 1990, an anonymous donation led to a new infield tarp and sprinkler system. In 1991–1992, bathrooms, concession stands and covered batting cages were also installed.

In 1997, the site of the former junior high was repurposed, and a baseball diamond, sports field and jogging track were built.

In 1999, money from the $49.95 million bond package funded major renovations to the high school, including classroom and cafeteria expansion, outdoor tennis courts, a softball field and a parking garage.

CONSTRUCTION OF FIRST NEW SCHOOL BUILDING IN 40 YEARS

- In 1992, with a $35.45 million bond election approved, a plan was finalized to build a new facility to house fifth through eighth grades.

- Land acquisition and construction cost $24 million.

- The new building opened in 1995 as two schools housed in one building with McCulloch Intermediate School serving fifth and sixth grades and Highland Park Middle School serving seventh and eighth grades. The 1,700 students shared a band hall, cafeteria, auditorium and library.

- The old building was demolished in 1997, and the school district published a commemorative booklet honoring the history of the school.

Above: A rendering of the new McCulloch Intermediate School and Highland Park Middle School.

Above right: HPMS teacher Yvonne Janik was photographed in The Dallas Morning News taking a picture of the demolition of McCulloch Middle School in 1997.

Economic and international ups and downs

The convergence of Internet usage, technological advances and the globalization of business and culture came together to create a newfound ability for everyday men and women to reach across continents in their day-to-day lives.

Nations became so profoundly interconnected that political, social and economic events created ripple effects that were felt instantly around the globe. The stock markets expanded for most of the decade before plummeting in the fall of 2008.

9/11 – A day that changed our world

The world watched in horror on Sept. 11, 2001, when terrorists flew two planes into the World Trade Center towers, a third into the Pentagon, and a fourth plane crashed into a field in Pennsylvania after its passengers overtook their captors. President George W. Bush declared a War on Terror, a war that knew no traditional boundaries or enemies.

Superintendent Dr. Cathy Bryce remembered when the news bulletins began to arrive.

"I was in an early morning meeting, and we heard the reports of what had happened. At first, it was that moment of, 'What is this? What is this, really?' And then when we got our arms and minds around what had happened, we immediately went into crisis management mode. We had training and procedures for that. We locked down our campuses initially, and we worked with city and town public safety officials to filter through what they were hearing about any possible threats to us here in Dallas.

Top left: Students pose for the traditional photo in front of the Robert S. Hyer sign.

Above: *Principal Dr. Gail Hartin poses with the UP Panther in 2000.*

Left: *Armstrong Principal Dr. Mary Richey recites the Pledge of Allegiance with kindergartners during morning announcements in 2001.*

CONSTRUCTION HIGHLIGHTS

- **2003:** A major four-year renovation of the high school was completed, and the new wing provided more classroom space and allowed for a new, larger cafeteria. The project also included the addition of outdoor tennis courts, a softball field and a parking garage.

- **2008–2010:** Highlights of projects funded by the 2008 bond issue:

  - Construction of additional classrooms

  - Replacement of portable classrooms with classrooms in the main buildings for all campuses

  - Safety measures, such as the purchase of security cameras and the configuration of front offices as mandatory check-in points for visitors

  - Expansion of repairs and maintenance to infrastructure needs, such as heating and air conditioning systems

  - Roofing replacements and repairs

  - Purchase of land behind the HPHS parking garage

  - Gym renovations on all campuses, including the addition of a competition gym at MIS/HPMS

  - Dining and kitchen expansions at all elementary schools

  - Artificial turf on the softball field

  - Technology upgrades and replacement for network infrastructure and data storage

  - Partial funding for the construction of a multi-purpose activities center at HPHS

  - Construction of the Business Services Annex at the Administration Building along with infrastructure updates and repairs

Top: *HPISD Trustees, administrators and parents watch as Armstrong students break ground for additions to the campus.*

Above right: *The Multi-Purpose Activities Center, opened in 2010, allows several HPHS teams and student groups the opportunity to practice indoors.*

Above left: *Portables were removed from UP Elementary, thanks to the 2008 bond issue.*

"Our focus was on keeping everyone safe and getting through the day. The bulk of our parents left their children with us that day, and any parents who wanted to pick up their children were able to do so right away. It was a comfort to know that our children were going home to loving families who would wrap their arms around them and try to make sense of what had happened that day.

"That day changed the way we think about school security. It made us focus in a new way on how to protect our campuses and how to keep our students and staff members safe," she said.

HPISD expands and aligns curriculum, technology

The decade marked a concerted effort to align curriculum, both vertically (in successive grades) and horizontally (across grades and, in the case of elementary schools, across campuses). Teachers worked together to ensure students were prepared for future years by embarking on intensive curriculum writing workshops over the summer. They also demonstrated their commitment to lifelong learning by participating in teaching conferences and writing institutes. In 2002, HPISD trustees voted to expand the kindergarten program to provide all–day instruction.

DR. CATHY BRYCE
HPISD'S SIXTH SUPERINTENDENT

In 2001, the School Board hired Dr. Cathy Bryce as its sixth superintendent. A native of Altus, Okla., Dr. Bryce was a lifelong educator who had served in leadership roles in many Dallas–Fort Worth schools. She came to Highland Park from Weatherford ISD.

Dr. Bryce was known for her strategic thinking, limitless energy and gift for communication. She was named Superintendent of the Year by the American Association of School Administrators in 2000 and Key Communicator of the Year by the Texas School Public Relations Association in 2008.

Dr. Bryce served as superintendent from 2001 to 2008. In 2014, Dr. Bryce was awarded the Highlander Award for the difference she made in HPISD.

Above: *In honor of her retirement, Texas State Rep. Dan Branch presents Superintendent Dr. Cathy Bryce with a flag that was flown over the Capitol.*

Left: *Armstrong students complete a group project in their learning loft.*

At the high school level, participation in challenging Advanced Placement courses skyrocketed. From 2000 to 2013, the number of students taking AP exams rose from 429 to 1,095, and the total number of exams taken grew from 997 to 2,719. In keeping with the commitment to prepare students for their future in the global workplace, the district introduced Mandarin Chinese as a foreign language class option.

As technology expanded its role in day–to–day life, HPISD decided to allow students to use their own devices in the classroom when teachers deemed it appropriate. Many teachers also introduced cell phone "parking lots," which were bins where students would put their phones when they weren't using them for research and learning.

Science Festival

Inspired by the Literary Festival, HP parent and chemical engineer Marie Naklie McCoy organized the first HPHS Science Festival in 2006.

During the one–day event, more than 50 speakers representing careers in science, technology, engineering and math visit the high school campus. These accomplished leaders discuss their careers, educational paths and work experience with students. All high school science students have the opportunity to engage in conversation and gain a deeper understanding of these vital and in–demand careers. Sponsored by the Science Department at Highland Park High School and organized by parent volunteers, the mission of the Science Festival is to encourage and inspire students to pursue careers in medicine, research, technology, engineering and science. The tradition continues today, with nearly 75 parent volunteers hosting the Science Festival each year.

A MIGHTY MERGER

In 2003, the Alumni Association merged with the Highland Park Education Foundation to form a single organization serving the needs of students, alumni, parents and friends of the school district.

Above: Bradfield Bronco buddies pose on the stairs in 2009.

Left: Dallas Cowboy Jason Witten thrilled students with a special visit to Bradfield Elementary in 2006.

Voters overwhelmingly approve $75.4 million bond issue

In 2008, HPISD voters overwhelmingly approved a $75.4 million school bond issue with 91.15 percent supporting the proposition.

"I am deeply grateful to the community for supporting the bond issue and for investing in the maintenance of the historical school houses that have served the students of HPISD for many decades," Dr. Bryce said. "We pledge to manage the money with the utmost care and to work closely with a community–based bond oversight committee to ensure that the projects are completed in accordance with community expectations."

HPISD School Board President Jeff Barnes called the results "a tremendous vote of confidence from our community."

DR. DAWSON ORR
HPISD'S SEVENTH SUPERINTENDENT

Dr. Dawson Orr served as Superintendent of Schools in Wichita Falls ISD before joining HPISD in 2009 as its seventh and current superintendent.

Dr. Orr is known as an articulate, thoughtful and respected leader. He has served as president of the Texas Association of School Administrators, chairperson of TASA's legislative committee and president of the Texas Leadership Center Board. He was named Superintendent of the Year by Communities in Schools in 2008 and Key Communicator of the Year by the Texas School Public Relations Association in 2005. He continues to serve as a member of TASA's legislative committee and the Visioning Institute, a study group made up of educational leaders focusing on school district redesign.

Left: *The Scots football team celebrates after winning the 2005 UIL 4A State Championship.*

Above: *HPHS alumni showed up in full force to support their Scots in the football championship game.*

2001

Dr. Cathy Bryce became HPISD's sixth superintendent

HPHS Alumni Association merged with HP Education Foundation

2003

HPISD School Board votes to limit class rank

The HPISD School Board voted to limit class rank in the fall of 2009. Under state law passed in 1997, school districts must rank the top 10 percent of their students because Texas public universities rely heavily on those numbers when making admissions decisions.

After hearing the report from a study committee, the HPISD School Board and HPISD administrators came to the consensus that the practice of ranking all students puts those students who are not in the top 10 percent of the class at a disadvantage.

The policy went into effect with the senior class of 2010. Parents and students overwhelmingly supported the change, and many Texas school districts followed HPISD's example by revising their class–ranking policies.

Top: *Ray Washburne, Class of 1979, refurbished and donated the original neon sign from the old Highlander Stadium, and it now hangs in the entrance of the current stadium.*

Above: *2009–10 HPISD Teachers of the Year and Hyer Principal Jeremy Gilbert hang out before a Rangers game with HP alum and Los Angeles Dodgers pitcher Clayton Kershaw.*

Left: *HPMS band students perform during the 2007 Shakespeare Festival.*

2006

HPHS Science Festival began

Dr. Dawson Orr became HPISD's seventh and current superintendent

2009

Leaders advocate for changes to state's school finance and mandatory testing systems

Superintendent Dr. Dawson Orr was hired in January 2009 following Dr. Bryce's retirement. He and the Board of Trustees rallied to advocate for school districts across Texas on two critical fronts: school finance and state–mandated standardized testing. In 2011, HPISD joined in a lawsuit over the school finance system. The Texas School Coalition, which is made up of revenue–contributing districts, challenged the constitutionality of the Texas school finance system, claiming that it fails to provide schools with sufficient funding to meet state educational standards, and that the system has become a statewide property tax. As of this writing, the lawsuit has not been resolved.

At the same time, Dr. Orr led a challenge regarding the increasing number of standardized tests required by the state.

"The tremendous work of Highland Park ISD principals and teachers to provide for academic excellence has continued, even in the face of ever–increasing bureaucratically driven mandatory testing," Dr. Orr said. "We need to fight to ensure that the learning environment that allows our students to excel is not eroded by a combined state and federal system that continues to require more standardized assessments."

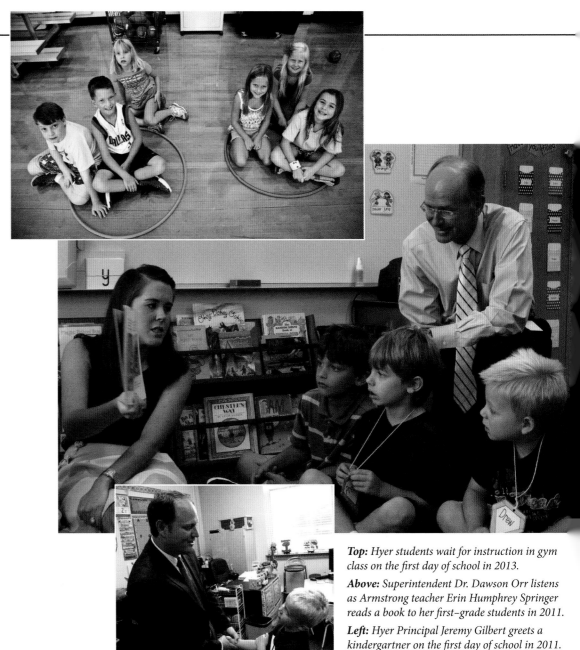

Top: *Hyer students wait for instruction in gym class on the first day of school in 2013.*

Above: *Superintendent Dr. Dawson Orr listens as Armstrong teacher Erin Humphrey Springer reads a book to her first–grade students in 2011.*

Left: *Hyer Principal Jeremy Gilbert greets a kindergartner on the first day of school in 2011.*

Dr. Orr, along with other superintendents in the North Texas Regional Consortium, a group of high–performing districts, continued to advocate for Texas schoolchildren by communicating with community members and state leaders about the detrimental effects of overtesting. As of this writing, HPISD is working to develop a community–based accountability and assessment system that is more effective than the state model.

Seven HP students get surprise visit from Bush at Presidential Library opening

On May 1, 2013, seven HPISD students were among the first 43 visitors at the George W. Bush Presidential Library and Museum. They were surprised and delighted when the former president himself greeted them in the Oval Office room.

"Welcome to the Oval Office," he said. "You're our first guests, and we're thrilled you're here."

Bush visited with 43 Dallas–area schoolchildren for more than 30 minutes, covering subjects ranging from a typical day at the White House to the profound role faith has played in his life.

Top left: *President George W. Bush made a surprise appearance at the opening of the Bush Presidential Library in 2013.*

Top right: *Seven HPISD students, one from each campus, were among the first 43 visitors to the new presidential library.*

Above: *Students enjoy lunch and conversation in the MIS/HPMS cafeteria.*

Bush intentionally requested that the first visitors be schoolchildren — not dignitaries or donors — because he wanted the Bush Center to be a place of learning.

Learners & Educators for the Future

In mapping out HPISD's path for the future, district leaders began with the most important person in mind: the student. The vision for preparing students to become tomorrow's leaders and responsible citizens led to the development of the profiles of the Learner for the Future and the Educator for the Future.

In 2012, the district assembled a study team made up of parents, students, teachers, administrators and university professors to identify the knowledge, skills, attributes and dispositions the HPISD student would need to become an accomplished person and lifelong learner. After months of study, discussion and collaboration, the team produced what you see today: the profile of the Learner for the Future. A similar team developed the profile of the Educator for the Future in 2013. The themes and goals embedded in those profiles continue to guide the district's work today.

LEARNER for the FUTURE

EDUCATOR for the FUTURE

Above: *Hyer students hang out in the hall on the first day of school in 2012.*

Left: *HPISD's vision for the learners and educators for the future continues to guide the district.*

September 24, 2010

District leaders mapped path for the future
with *Learner for the Future* profile

*Multi–Purpose Activities
Center opened*

2012

Superintendent Dr. Dawson Orr watches as Bradfield students head to the cafeteria.

2013

HPISD marked its centennial

Educator for the Future
profile published

October 12, 2014

HPISD sets new enrollment record, HPHS moves up to 6A

HPISD's enrollment hit a new high of 7,022 students in the fall of 2013. The district was growing at all levels, including the high school, which was reclassified in the 6A large high school division, a change that took effect in 2014.

"The Scots are always competitive," Superintendent Dr. Dawson Orr said. "We look forward to the challenge."

Although the funding supplied by the 2008 bond issue allowed the district to add square footage and eliminate portable classrooms, the steady growth quickly filled that space. Once again, Highland Park ISD trustees studied the best strategies for serving the growing student enrollment in a 6.2–square–mile densely developed and populated area. The growth is a testament to HPISD's reputation of excellence, which continues to attract new families.

Top: The HPHS Bagpipers practice before performing at the Superintendent's Convocation in August 2013.

Above: Superintendent Dr. Dawson Orr and MIS/HPMS Cafeteria Manager Brenda Vardell cut the ribbon during the opening of the remodeled cafeteria in 2014.

Left: An Armstrong kindergartner multitasks with a book and headphones in 2011.

Class of 2013 graduates celebrate at their commencement ceremony.

Celebrating the past and hailing the future

While it is not possible to capture a century of stories in one book, the small mosaic collected here reflects what is possible when a community joins hands with its schools. Over the years since 1914, the students educated in Highland Park ISD have gone on to lead lives rich in opportunity, experiences and leadership. They have truly entered to learn and have gone forth to serve in every possible arena.

"The enduring legacy of this district is found in the families that for generations have contributed to excellence, whether academic, athletic, artistic or in the spirit of service," Dr. Orr said. "We celebrate the past, recognizing all the traditions that have been built over the years and the outstanding individuals upon whose shoulders we stand today."

"When I look back to the 1924 *Highlander*, I am struck by the wisdom of the members of the senior class who wrote, 'Many schools live merely on the momentum and traditions they have gathered in the more flourishing days of past. We are proud of our short past, but we are prouder of the Highland Park High School that is to be.'" Dr. Orr said.

"Just like those 1924 graduates, we hail the future, looking forward to seeing what today's kindergartners will go on to do as they continue to write this remarkable story."

As we celebrate a century of excellence, we harken back to those words that have inspired generations of Scots:

Enter to Learn
Go Forth to Serve

Andrew Barnes, Class of 2012, and his grandfather, Art Barnes, Class of 1951, proudly display their Blanket Awards. The National Honor Society awards the blankets annually to a senior boy and girl who most exemplify scholarship, character, leadership and service.

Academic Excellence,
Traditions
and
Campuses

Academic Excellence

The word tradition rings long and clear across Highland Park ISD. Intertwined with tradition is the commitment to academic excellence. This commitment comes from the students who are charting their course and the teachers and leaders who set the bar high, both inside and outside the classroom.

In this section, you will find snapshots that reflect a journey of 100 years. That journey includes traditions ranging from bagpipers dancing atop drums to pep rallies that show off the many talents of so many young people. But whatever the campus or activity, there is no doubt that traditions give us all a sense of HP pride.

Top right: *Anne Hoopingarner, Class of 1957, shows off her Blanket Award.*

Bottom right: *Thomas Cotton, Class of 1961, and Melissa McCoy, Class of 2008, are the two HPHS graduates to receive the prestigious Rhodes Scholarship.*

Right: *HPHS students complete a science experiment in 2013.*

Top left: *The 1939 National Honor Society poses for a photo.*

Left: *The 1953 National Honor Society officers proudly surround the symbol of their club.*

Bottom left: *The 1971–72 National Merit Semifinalists take time from studying to take a photo on a fire engine.*

Below: *The 1972–73 National Honor Society lights the ceremonial candle during initiation.*

Top: *The 1955 Blanket Award winners beam with pride.*
Above: *Members of the 1932 National Honor Society take a photo in front of the school.*

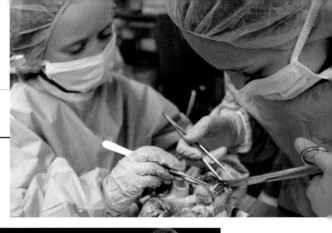

Top left: *Bradfield's 2006 Biography Day.*

Top center: *HPHS Principal Patrick Cates with top students from the Class of 2007.*

Top right: *Armstrong TAG students dissect a hog's heart.*

Right: *Bradfield's 2006 Biography Day.*

Far right: *MIS/HPMS Principal Dr. Laurie Hitzelberger congratulates a student at the 2010 awards ceremony.*

Bottom left: *Universities around the nation honored HPHS juniors with book awards in 2012.*

Bottom right: *The HPHS Science Team won its eighth consecutive UIL State Championship in 2013.*

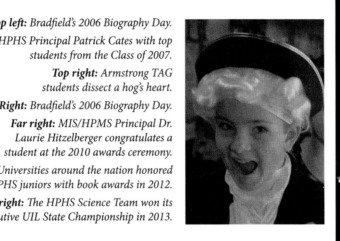

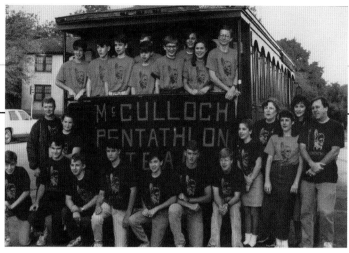

Top left: *The National Junior Honor Society hosts an annual ceremony at the middle school.*

Top right: *The McCulloch Middle School Academic Pentathlon team from the late '80s.*

Left: *The HPHS Robotics Club finishes work on a robot for a competition in 2013.*

Bottom right: *Members of the UP Elementary Chess Club hone their skills before the school day begins.*

Bottom left: *McCulloch Intermediate School hosts a Spelling Bee.*

Traditions

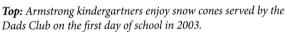

Top: HPHS seniors put their creativity on display by painting a hallway each year.

Above: Hyer moms entertain students and faculty during a 1981 skit.

Right: Linda Browne Otstott performs the traditional Highlander Fling dance atop a drum.

Top: Armstrong kindergartners enjoy snow cones served by the Dads Club on the first day of school in 2003.

Center left: Middle school students graduate from the D.A.R.E. program in 2006.

Center right: Former Dallas Cowboys Head Coach Tom Landry visits McCulloch Middle School in 1995 for Career Day.

Above: Armstrong Principal Dr. Mary Richey serves cake to students during a fall picnic.

Left: Hyer students play tug-of-war during the 2010 field day competition.

Below: Bradfield girls have a smashing time with their confetti eggs at the 2009 fall carnival.

Bottom right: Each elementary school acknowledges grandparents with special presentations every year.

Bottom left: HPHS seniors welcome kindergartners by giving them a T-shirt with their year of graduation on the first day of school.

Top right: Parents cover the HPHS campus in yellow ribbons when a team heads to the playoffs.

Top: Bradfield students sort letters for the writing project Bronco Express.

Above: The HPHS Drum Line performs during the annual black light pep rally.

Above: *The Robert S. Hyer sign has been a popular photo spot for many years.*

Top left: *UP Elementary students learn about different cultures during International Day.*

Top right: *Pucker up! A Hyer grandparent is shown love during Grandfriends Day.*

Center right: *A football player proudly displays his victory apple during a pep rally.*

Center left: *A senior hands the first day T-shirt to a Hyer kindergartner.*

Bottom right: *Hyer fourth graders are cheered on as they run down the halls for the end-of-the-year Clap Out celebration.*

Bottom left: *UP students celebrate Arbor Day 2013 by planting a tree.*

Top: *The Scotsmen pump up the crowd during a pep rally.*
Top right: *UP students at the Bike Rodeo.*
Center: *The Raider Band performs a special concert on Veterans Day.*
Above: *Fifth graders head to Sky Ranch for an annual science adventure.*
Left: *Students navigate the halls with their pack of supplies at MIS/HPMS.*
Far left: *UP students at the annual Bike Rodeo.*

Campuses — Armstrong Elementary

John S. Armstrong
Parent-Teacher
Association

Highland
Park

Organized
November 19, 1914

"The Love of Childhood is the Common Tie Which Should Unite Us in Holiest Purpose."

Top left: *A class photo from 1928.*

Top center: *A class photo from 1943.*

Top right: *The John S. Armstrong PTA was founded Nov. 19, 1914.*

Left: *First-graders pose for a class photo in 1950.*

Far left: *Students pose for a class photo in 1933.*

Principals

1914	1917	1920	1938
Belle Francis	*C. P. Hudson*	*H. B. Howard*	*J. Bayles Earle*

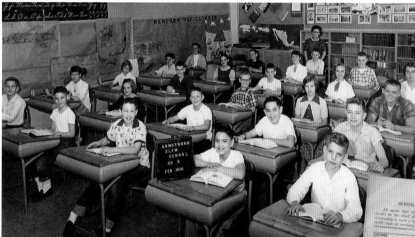

Top left: *The 1953 orchestra.*

Top right: *The new John S. Armstrong campus reopened in 1953 to replace the previous building that burned down.*

Center: *Sixth-graders take a photo in their classroom in 1956.*

Bottom right: *A monthly report card from 1936.*

Right: *Students give a presentation in the library in 1965.*

Center left: *A group of girls observes as a boy learns how to shave in 1962.*

1945

Ralph B. Griffin

1978

Dr. Kenneth Thomas

1996

Dr. Mary Richey

2011

Dr. Skip Moran

Armstrong Elementary

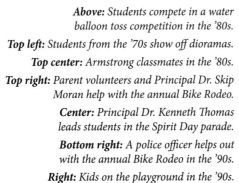

Above: Students compete in a water balloon toss competition in the '80s.

Top left: Students from the '70s show off dioramas.

Top center: Armstrong classmates in the '80s.

Top right: Parent volunteers and Principal Dr. Skip Moran help with the annual Bike Rodeo.

Center: Principal Dr. Kenneth Thomas leads students in the Spirit Day parade.

Bottom right: A police officer helps out with the annual Bike Rodeo in the '90s.

Right: Kids on the playground in the '90s.

Top left: *Fourth-graders perform a concert with recorders.*

Top right: *A mother and daughter on the first day of school in 2012.*

Center left: *Kindergartners show off their Halloween costumes.*

Center: *Armstrong Eagles show off their green and gold pride on Spirit Day.*

Center right: *Principal Dr. Skip Moran greets a student on the first day of school in 2012.*

Above left: *Students in the PAWS program are committed to being leaders in their school.*

Above right: *Armstrong hosts a fiesta in 2002.*

Left: *Fathers and sons carry on Armstrong's winning spirit on the baseball diamond.*

Bradfield Elementary

Top left: *First-graders in 1943.*

Top center: *A class photo from 1935.*

Top right: *Students dress up as vegetables for a play in 1950.*

Far left: *Students celebrate America's birth with Colonial Days in 1963.*

Center: *A third-grade class from 1950.*

Above: *Neighborhood kids from Bradfield dress up as cowboys to protect the town from outlaws in 1935.*

Left: *A class photo from the '50s.*

Principals

1927
J. F.
Harris

1936
Howard
Chapman

1946
Melvin G.
Marks

1958
William T.
Bryant

1968
Noble
Atkins

Top left: *Students celebrate America's bicentennial by dressing as colonists and a bald eagle in 1976.*

Top center: *A class photo from the 1975–76 school year.*

Top right: *Bradfield hosts a 50th birthday celebration in 1976.*

Far right: *Parents and students enjoy a campus picnic in the 2000s.*

Right: *Bradfield Broncos enjoyed their new playground and sport court in the 2000s.*

Center: *Students play hide-and-go-seek in the '90s.*

1978

Joseph P.
Koenig

1982

Elaine
Prude

1994

Jaynie
Milner

1998

Dr. Gloria
McNutt

2012

Chris
Brunner

Bradfield Elementary

Top left: *Students head home after a fun-filled first day of school.*

Top center: *Bradfield loves to help charitable organizations, like the Salvation Army.*

Center right: *Passing planes could see Bradfield's enthusiasm for the 100th day of school in 2014.*

Right: *Lifelong friendships are built in elementary school.*

Above left: *Bradfield students visited the WFAA studios in 2013.*

Top left: Students create Dale Chihuly–inspired artwork from recycled items in 2013.

Top right: Kindergartners show off their new shirts on the first day of school.

Above: Bradfield students love to read!

Left: Principal Chris Brunner greets students with a gift and a smile on the first day of school in 2013.

Hyer Elementary

Bottom left: *A classroom at Hyer in the '60s.*

Top left: *First-graders in 1958.*

Top center: *Students in front of the school during the 1948–49 school year.*

Top right: *Hyer students pose for a class photo in the '60s.*

Center: *Parents watch as their children perform a choir concert in the '60s.*

Bottom center: *Camp Fire Girls take a photo in front of the Hyer sign in 1973.*

Above: *A 1960s Hyer classroom.*

Principals

1949
Newton
Manning

1973
Tom
Munroe

1982
Dale
Lawrence

Above: *Hyer students show off their skills during field day in 1981.*

Top center: *Students dress as historical figures for the 1982 Biography Day.*

Far right: *Principal Dr. Louis Powers helps kick off a gift wrap fundraiser during the 1996–97 school year.*

Bottom right: *A certificate from the Texas Readers Club, issued to a Hyer student in 1976.*

Right: *Second-graders in the 2003–04 school year.*

Center: *Students lower the flag on the last day of school in 2002.*

1985

Dr. Louis Powers

2003

Greg Smith

2008

Jeremy Gilbert

Hyer Elementary

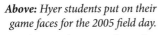

Above: *Hyer students put on their game faces for the 2005 field day.*

Top center: *Hyer students at the 2004 Bike Rodeo.*

Bottom right: *2013 Bike Rodeo Safety Chair Kandi Tanner presents fourth-grader Alexa Magee with a new bike for winning the T-shirt art contest.*

Bottom center: *Students spend a week perfecting their writing skills during Camp Write Along in 2014.*

Center: *A proud student shows off a note from his mom on the first day of school in 2013.*

Top left: *Hyer moms get in the game for the fourth-grade Moms Skit in 2003.*

Top center: *A student jumps for joy — and a gold medal — in the Field Day sack race.*

Above: *Picture perfect: a first-grader smiles on the first day of school in 2012.*

Bottom center: *Hyer students are proud to be Huskies for life.*

Center: *Hyer's first four principals gather in front of the school during a ceremony.*

Bottom left: *Playing a game in the Husky gym in 2013.*

University Park Elementary

Top left: *A class photo in front of the school in 1949.*

Top center: *A Camp Fire Girls meeting in 1955.*

Above: *Sixth-graders practice their piano skills in 1962.*

Bottom center: *Students stay active during gym class in 1962.*

Bottom left: *A 1953 class photo.*

Principals

1928
Joe P. Harris

1934 *1937*
Warren P. Herring
Stanley Clifton

1938
Herman G. Williams

1965
Elton Tielke

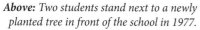

Above: Two students stand next to a newly planted tree in front of the school in 1977.

Top center: Students in 1985.

Top right: Principal Dr. Lynda Carter meets with Derrill Elmore, who attended first grade at UP in 1928.

Right center: Fourth-graders practice the recorder in the 2011–12 school year.

Bottom right: A Park Cities News *photo of the four UP principals who spanned six decades at the school.*

Bottom center: Superintendent Dr. Dawson Orr and Principal Dr. Lynda Carter honor the Principals for the Day.

Center: Duck! Students play dodgeball during the 2011–12 school year.

Principled Principals

University Park Elementary kicked-off its 60th birthday celebration with a reception honoring faculty, past and present of the school. Pictured are four who have served as principal for the school. Standing left to right are: H.G. Williams, 1938-65; Dr. Elton Tielke, 1965-70; Dr. Tom Parker, 1972-75. Seated is Dr. Charles Cole who arrived in 1985.

Park Cities News photo by Lee Zethraus

ACADEMIC EXCELLENCE, TRADITIONS AND CAMPUSES

1970

Winston Power

1972

Tom Parker

1975

Dr. Rodney Pirtle

1985

Dr. Charles Cole

1990

Dr. Gail Hartin

2003

Dr. Lynda Carter

81

University Park Elementary

Above: *A student shows off his winning artwork for a calendar contest.*

Top center: *UP celebrated its 85th birthday in 2013.*

Far right: *Students practice their bicycle safety skills during a recent Bike Rodeo.*

Bottom right: *Students host the morning announcements on KPAW TV.*

Bottom: *The UP Elementary Outdoor Learning Plaza opened in 2011.*

Center: *Grandparents serve healthy lunches in 2014.*

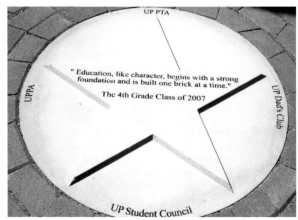

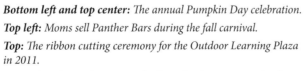

Bottom left and top center: *The annual Pumpkin Day celebration.*

Top left: *Moms sell Panther Bars during the fall carnival.*

Top: *The ribbon cutting ceremony for the Outdoor Learning Plaza in 2011.*

Top right: *The Student Council officers for the 2013–14 school year.*

Bottom right: *A special marker on campus, donated by the fourth-grade class of 2007.*

Bottom center: *Students line up to show their excitement for the 85th birthday of UP Elementary.*

McCulloch Intermediate School & Highland Park Middle School

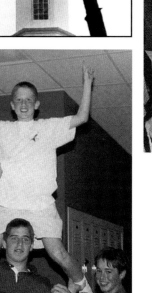

Above: *The first staff of McCulloch Intermediate School in 1995.*

Top center: *Principals Dr. Linda Salinas and Robert Dyer lead a tour during the construction of the new MIS/HPMS campus in 1995.*

Top right: *The cupola is lowered into place.*

Far right: *Eighth-graders show off their dance moves in 1998.*

Bottom right: *Boys goofing off in the hallways of HPMS in 1997.*

Right: *MIS students in 1997 know the right answers.*

Principals
McCulloch Intermediate School

1995

Dr. Linda Salinas

1996

Dr. Caren Edelstein

2003

Dr. Laurie Hitzelberger

Above: Middle school safety patrol students stand guard in 1998.

Top center: HPMS students enjoy a moment outside the campus in 2003.

Top right: Fifth-graders make a pyramid in the hallway in 2003.

Bottom right: HP graduates Nancy Burgher and Julie Ann O'Connell share their experiences as children during World War II with MIS students in 2013.

Bottom center: The Class of 2018 is already counting down the years to graduation.

Center: Friends gather for a photo in 2003.

Principals
Highland Park Middle School

1995

Barbara
Beeler

2002

Dr. Kimbroly
Pool

2005

Dr. Laurie
Hitzelberger

McCulloch Intermediate School & Highland Park Middle School

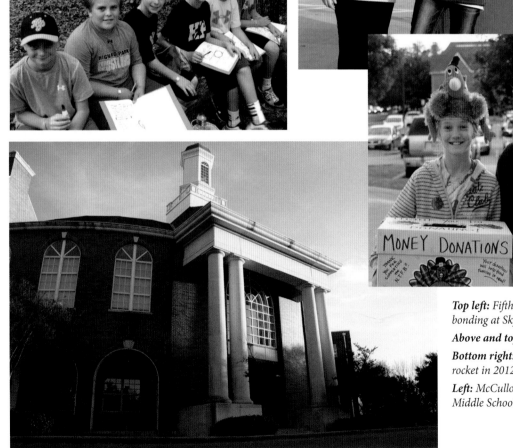

Top left: *Fifth-graders have a great time learning and bonding at Sky Ranch in 2013.*

Above and top: *Students support the turkey drive in 2014.*

Bottom right: *The finishing touches are put on a model rocket in 2012.*

Left: *McCulloch Intermediate School and Highland Park Middle School opened in the fall of 1995, serving grades 5–8.*

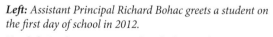

Left: *Assistant Principal Richard Bohac greets a student on the first day of school in 2012.*

Top left: *Students memorize their locker combinations on the first day of school.*

Top: *A distinguished group celebrates the groundbreaking of the new MIS/HPMS campus.*

Top right: *Superintendent Dr. Dawson Orr visits a classroom in 2012.*

Bottom right: *Principal Dr. Laurie Hitzelberger enjoys a laugh with her students.*

Above: *Fifth-graders are hams, especially in the cafeteria.*

Highland Park Junior High School (1937–1970)
Highland Park Middle School (1970–1974)
Arch H. McCulloch Middle School (1974–1995)

Top left: *A member of the HP Junior High band and his director in 1966.*

Top center: *Students in HP Junior High School in 1948.*

Top right: *Students practice their sewing skills in home economics class in 1967.*

Left: *An honor awards ceremony in 1961.*

Principals

1936

John F. Harris

1950

Pat Woosley

1966

Cecil L. Redd

Left: *Band practice in 1968.*
Top: *The 1968 Fire Captains.*
Far right: *A copy of* The Chieftain, *the student handbook in 1969.*
Right: *The winners of the name contest and cover design contest for* The Tribesman.
Above: *A tennis lesson in gym class in 1969.*

1978

Cecil
Floyd

1993

Robert
Dyer

1994

Dr. Linda
Salinas

Left: *A Valentine's Day dance in 1978.*
Top left: *Students show their support for the Red Raiders in 1969.*
Top right: *Eighth-graders show up for a special breakfast in 1988.*
Bottom right: *Students show off the fashions of the '80s.*
Center: *An eighth-grade classroom photo from 1972–73.*

HIGHLAND PARK JR. H.S. RED RAIDERS

Left: *Club and team representatives in front of McCulloch Middle School in 1994.*

Far left: *A patch from HP Junior High School.*

Above: *The original high school building was converted to Highland Park Junior High School in 1937. It was renamed Highland Park Middle School in 1970, and then dedicated as Arch H. McCulloch Middle School in 1974.*

Highland Park High School

Bottom left: *HPHS diploma from 1940.*

Top left: *Students hanging out on the front steps of the school in 1928.*

Above: *Lou Smith was voted Most Popular Girl in 1928.*

Left: *J. B. Hudnall was voted Best All Round Boy in 1929.*

Center: *Jim and Claire Roberts after the 1953 commencement ceremony.*

Principals

 *1924*
Eugene S. Lawler

 *1928*
Ben W. Wiseman

 *1963*
C. D. Bowlby

 *1966*
Everett Hart

Top left: *A student uses a tape recorder in 1962.*

Top center: *A graduation party in 1956 at the Dallas Country Club.*

Top right: *Seniors show off their 'staches in 1955.*

Above: *A student receives her diploma in 1956.*

Left: *Class officers in 1955.*

Bottom center: *The 1963 Homecoming Queen is crowned.*

Bottom left: *Students are excited to leave class in 1964.*

1973
Dr. E. A. Sigler

1982
Tom Munroe

1986
Jim Gibson

1990
Don O'Quinn

1993
Dr. Linda Salinas (Interim)

Highland Park High School

Top left: *Girls wave from a convertible in 1964.*

Top right: *Seniors build a snowman in 1964.*

Center right: *Students shoe polish a car in 1977.*

Bottom right: *A student clicks his heels on the way out the door in 1977.*

Center: *1975 graduating seniors — future Armstrong PTA President Linda Roberts Sommerville and future Board Member Cynthia Beecherl.*

Bottom center: *Boys calling for a date in 1977.*

Far left: *Girls ride their bikes to school in 1964.*

1994
Jean
Rutherford

1998
Bob
Albano

2000
Robert Jolly
(Interim)

2002
Patrick
Cates

2010
Walter
Kelly

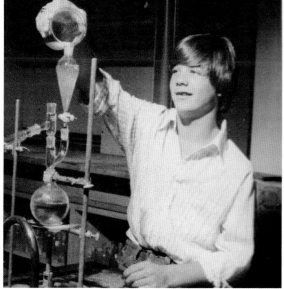

Above: *Students hanging out in 1977.*

Top center: *Principal Walter Kelly observes a classroom in 2013.*

Top right: *Students sit with a Scottie on the bench, donated in 2014 in honor of the centennial.*

Far right: *A student conducts a science experiment in 1977.*

Right: *Students collect data in the science lab in 2011.*

Bottom right: *Freshmen collect their textbooks during Fish Camp Orientation.*

Below: *A HP boy shows off his dedication to the school in 1989.*

Head Football Coach Randy Allen and his team reflect during the National Anthem before a game.

Athletics, Extracurricular Activities *and* Clubs

Everyone knows there is more to student life than what goes on in the classroom. Teams and clubs that appeal to each individual are an integral part of learning and growing up.

In this section, you'll find Eagles, Broncos, Huskies, Panthers, Raiders and Scots doing what they love best and doing it in style, whether they're on the playing field, the performance stage or at the chess board. Our campuses not only offer our students the chance to compete with others in UIL events, but they also have clubs dedicated to interests ranging from robotics to ultimate Frisbee.

Friday Night Lights

During a Friday night in autumn, Highlander Stadium doesn't belong to one team or group of students. It transforms into a community celebration, awash in blue and gold. The combination of sounds from the football field, roars from the crowd, music from the band and pipers, cheers from the cheerleaders and Scotsmen and the beat of the Belles dance routine creates a thrilling atmosphere for all.

Longtime community photographer Brad Bradley is honored during halftime of a football game.

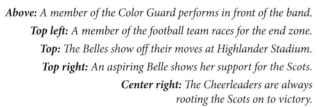

Above: *A member of the Color Guard performs in front of the band.*

Top left: *A member of the football team races for the end zone.*

Top: *The Belles show off their moves at Highlander Stadium.*

Top right: *An aspiring Belle shows her support for the Scots.*

Center right: *The Cheerleaders are always rooting the Scots on to victory.*

Bottom right: *The sounds of the bagpipes ring true at home football games.*

Bottom center: *The Scotsmen rally the crowd by running flags across the field after a score.*

Football

Since its inception in 1923, the Highland Park Scot football team has been a powerhouse in the football-rich lands of Texas. As of 2013, the Scots have won 767 games, the most of any team in Texas high school football history, and own three state championships. The Scots have produced many professional football players, including two Pro Football Hall of Famers, Doak Walker and Bobby Layne, and the number one overall pick in the 2009 NFL Draft, Matthew Stafford. Before donning the blue and gold, many young HP students play competitive football in YMCA leagues and for the HPMS Raiders.

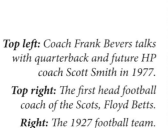

Top left: Coach Frank Bevers talks with quarterback and future HP coach Scott Smith in 1977.
Top right: The first head football coach of the Scots, Floyd Betts.
Right: The 1927 football team.

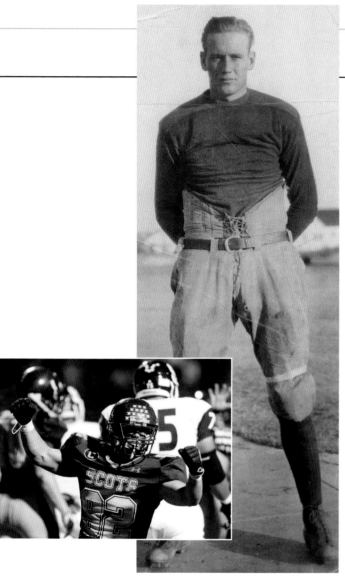

Above left: *Tanner Houghton celebrates after a big play.*
Above: *Alfred "Big 'Un" Rose, Class of 1926, was inducted in to the Texas High School Football Hall of Fame.*
Top: *The Scots look to score during a 2013 playoff game at AT&T Stadium.*
Top right: *A young football star at HPMS in 2013.*
Far right: *A playoff game program from 1977.*
Center: *Members of the 1949 football team.*
Bottom center: *Football players take a dive in 1980.*

HIGHLAND PARK VS. PLANO

50¢

DECEMBER 3, 1977
TEXAS STADIUM

QUARTER-FINALS

Baseball

Highland Park has participated in America's Pastime since the high school opened in 1922. The Scots won the state championship in 1997 — 98 and were led by pitcher Chris Young, who would go on to pitch in the major leagues. The team can also count Clayton Kershaw as one of its star alumni. Kershaw was drafted seventh overall in the 2006 MLB Draft by the Los Angeles Dodgers and has since won two Cy Young Awards for being the best pitcher in the National League.

Below: *Players listening to their coach in 1974.*
Top: *A pitcher in 1991.*
Right: *Players and coaches from the 1957 baseball squad.*

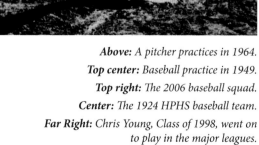

Above: A pitcher practices in 1964.
Top center: Baseball practice in 1949.
Top right: The 2006 baseball squad.
Center: The 1924 HPHS baseball team.
Far Right: Chris Young, Class of 1998, went on
to play in the major leagues.
Right: Clayton Kershaw, Class of 2006, has won two
Cy Young Awards in his career with the Los Angeles Dodgers.
(photo: Jon SooHoo, Los Angeles Dodgers)

Softball

Softball was an intramural girls sport for many years at Highland Park High School. The first official team to participate in district competition was formed in 1994, and the team continues to grow to this day. In 2013, the City of University Park passed a proposal to allow the installation of lights at the softball field, allowing both JV and varsity teams to play at the same site, even after dark. The team celebrated with a "let there be light" ceremony in 2014.

Top: *The 1955 intramural softball team.*
Bottom: *The 1996 varsity softball team.*

Above: The Lady Scots get defensive.
Top left: Members of the 2014 softball team.
Top: The 2014 varsity softball team.
Center: Jerry Sutterfield, former Girls Athletic Director, had an integral role in getting field lights installed for the softball team in 2014.
Bottom: The Lady Scots in 2014.

Boys Basketball

Boys have been playing competitive basketball in HPISD as far back as 1918, before the original high school was even built. Many things have changed on the court, including the addition of the 3-point line and the length of gym shorts, but the Scots continue to field a competitive and exciting team on the court each year. The Scots have won 33 district championships and finished second in the state title game to Houston Waltrip in 1998. Before becoming Scots, many seventh and eighth graders play for the Highland Park Middle School Raiders.

Top: *The 1924 boys basketball team.*
Bottom: *The 2013–14 basketball team.*

Above: Coach Bo Snowden and
his team captains in 1982.
Top center: The Scots shoot a free throw in 1974.
Far right: The Scots shoot for the basket in 1977.
Center: The eighth-grade Raiders in 2014.
Bottom center: A Scot surveys the defense in 2008.
Bottom left: Going for a layup in 1983.

Girls Basketball

Basketball has been a popular sport for girls in HP, dating back to at least 1918 at John S. Armstrong School. But up until the late '80s, it largely remained an intramural sport. During the 1986–87 school year, the Lady Scots basketball team entered varsity competition. Only two players on the inaugural team completed the preseason team training, while the remainder of the players joined the team at the end of their volleyball season. The sport has grown in popularity and now features a JV, freshman, and seventh- and eighth-grade teams. The varsity squad has appeared in the playoffs every year since 2008.

Top: The girls basketball team in 1924.
Bottom left: The girls team in 2014.
Bottom right: The Lady Scots in 1987.

Above: The 1996–97 team seniors.
Top left: The HPMS Lady Raiders in 2014.
Top center: The Lady Scots host Forney in a 2014 game.
Far right: Girls played basketball in gym class in 1943.
Bottom right: An intramural team from 1954.

Boys Cross Country

The boys cross country team began operating independently during the 1968–69 school year. The squad was previously a division of track and field. The original team practiced at White Rock Lake, Caruth Park and Fretz Park in far north Dallas, running more than 10 miles a day. The team has won several district and regional championships, and many students have represented HP at the UIL state meet.

Right: Members of the first cross country team from 1968.
Far right: The 2000 cross country team sprints off the line.

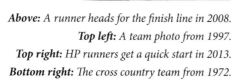

Above: A runner heads for the finish line in 2008.
Top left: A team photo from 1997.
Top right: HP runners get a quick start in 2013.
Bottom right: The cross country team from 1972.

Girls Cross Country

The girls cross country team burst onto the scene in 1975, the same year that the UIL recognized the sport for girls. From 1975 to 2013, the Lady Scots won 35 district championships, 32 regional championships and 14 UIL state titles. The Lady Scots have won more state titles than any other girls team in Texas. Four HP girls also own individual gold medals at the state championship: Crystal McGuire in 1984, Emily Field in 1998, Sara Sutherland in 2007 and Natalie Rathjen in 2013. The program is as strong as ever, boasting more than 130 members on the team. If you see a group of girls running before the sun has come up, it's likely they're just training for the next state title.

Above: A runner clears an obstacle in 2000.
Center: The Lady Scots show off their trophies in 1983.
Top right: The Lady Scots listen to advice from Coach Jerry Sutterfield.

Above: *State champion Sara Sutherland shows off her medal with her coaches.*

Top: *The Lady Scots during a competition in 2011.*

Far right: *Coach Jerry Sutterfield helped bolster the popularity of the girls cross country program at HPHS.*

Center: *The Lady Scots congratulate each other after a race in 2013.*

Bottom right: *The Lady Scots lead the pack at a race in 2008.*

Boys Golf

The boys golf team dates back to the 1930–31 school year at Highland Park High School. The team has won 18 UIL state championships during that span, including seven consecutive from 2000 to 2006, a state record. HP has a record nine UIL individual state championships, including two apiece from Cody Gribble and Trip Kuehne, and three consecutive championships by Scottie Scheffler from 2012 to 2014.

Top right: Teammates analyze a swing in 1943.
Bottom right: Scottie Scheffler won three consecutive UIL State Championships from 2012 to 2014.
Bottom left: The golf team in 1972.

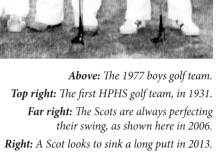

Above: The 1977 boys golf team.
Top right: The first HPHS golf team, in 1931.
Far right: The Scots are always perfecting their swing, as shown here in 2006.
Right: A Scot looks to sink a long putt in 2013.

Girls Golf

The first girls golf team appeared on the links during the 1976–77 school year, with four girls on the first roster. Since then, the team has captured four UIL state titles, including the most recent in 2008. An incredible feat was accomplished by 1995 HP grad Kelli Kuehne when she won four straight individual championships. Kuehne never lost a tournament that she entered while at HP, and she also won the U.S. Junior Girls Championship, one of the biggest tournaments in the world.

Right: A member of the golf team in 1977.
Top: A member of the golf team in 1995.
Far right: The first girls golf team was formed in 1977.
Bottom: Girls hit the links in 1983.

The girls golf team in 1998, coached by HPISD Planetarium Director Donna Pierce.

Boys Gymnastics

The boys gymnastics program was founded at Highland Park High School during the 1978–79 school year, and the team won the state championship in 1995. The Scots have had several members win individual state championships, including All-Around champions Adam Forman, Peter Hegi, Graham Cathey and Meyer Williams, who won gold medals in all six events during his junior year. The boys gymnastics program has captured 30 district titles.

Bottom: *Coach Mark Sherman spots a student during a flip.*
Top: *A student performs a balancing act in 2006.*
Far right: *An athlete shows his skills on the rings in 1987.*

Above: *A team photo from 1983.*
Top right: *Gymnasts Meyer Williams and Arielle Iola show off their gold medals from the 2013 THSGCA state championship.*
Right: *An athlete practices on the rings in 2006.*

Girls Gymnastics

The girls gymnastics squad was founded at the same time as the boys, in 1978–79. The girls made their first, and best, showing at the state championship in 1994, when they placed third as a team. Kimiyo Brown, 2006 grad, was the first girl from HP to be selected to the national high school team. Arielle Iola, 2013 HPHS graduate, won back-to-back All-Around gold medals in the 2012 and 2013 state championship meets, and she earned four gold medals for individual events during her career at the state meets.

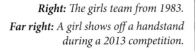

Right: The girls team from 1983.
Far right: A girl shows off a handstand during a 2013 competition.

Left: *An athlete performs a routine in 1991.*
Top: *The boys and girls teams in 1991.*
Above: *A boys and girls team photo in 1983.*

Boys Soccer

Competitive soccer first formed in HP during the 1974–75 school year. The team advanced to the UIL state championship game in 1987, finishing in second place with a 0-1 loss to San Antonio Alamo Heights. Although soccer was not a school-sponsored sport while he was at HPHS, 1968 grad Kyle Rote, Jr. is one of the best players in U.S. soccer history. He led the North American Soccer League in scoring in 1973 and was inducted into the National Soccer Hall of Fame in 2010.

Top: *The Scots go for the goal in 1982.*
Right: *The boys soccer team in 1977.*

Above: *The Scots goalie makes a diving stop in 2000.*
Top left: *An athlete keeps his eye on the ball in 1983.*
Top right: *The 2010–11 varsity soccer team.*
Bottom right: *The 1984 team captains.*

Girls Soccer

The Lady Scots soccer team started during the 1977–78 school year, and during its relatively short history has already added five UIL state championships and three second-place finishes to its resume. The years in which the Lady Scots have added championship hardware to the HP trophy case include 1994, 1996, 2000, 2002, and they ended a 10-year drought with a state title in 2012.

Right: *An athlete juggles the ball in 2013.*
Top: *The girls soccer team in 1983.*
Bottom: *A player dribbles the ball down the pitch in 2006.*

Above: The Lady Scots keep their head in the game in 2013.

Top: The Lady Scots won the UIL State Championship in 2012, and finished as runners-up in 2013.

Center: The 1984 girls soccer team.

Far right: A senior goes for the goal in 1983.

Bottom: The 1984 varsity team captains.

Swimming and Diving

The HP Swimming and Diving team originally began as a boys sport in 1941 and was known as the Aquatics Club. It dropped the club name in 1945 and added girls to the sport in 1953. The boys team earned one UIL state championship in 1999–2000. The girls team has dominated the 21st century, winning 12 UIL state titles from 2001 to 2013. The Scots have also won countless gold medals during individual competitions at the state championship meets. Four HP swimming and diving alumni have gone on to win Olympic gold medals: Skippy Browning, '48 grad; Bruce Hayes, '81 grad; Mike Heath, '82 grad; and Shaun Jordan, '86 grad.

Top: Coach Jerry Culp talks to his Scot swimmers during practice in the early 60s.
Right: The Highland Park girls team in 1964.

Top left: *Nancy Sanford listens to training tips from Coach Douglas Scherer.*

Top right: *The 2013–14 boys team celebrates its regional championship victory.*

Bottom right: *Meredith Higgins waits for the buzzer before the race begins in 2006.*

Right: *A swimmer perfects the backstroke in 1949.*

Tennis

The Highland Park tennis program is consistently ranked among the best in the state. In 2013, the tennis team won a state record 15th UIL state championship, its sixth consecutive. From 1988 to 2013, the Scots tennis team qualified for 26 consecutive UIL state championship tournaments, a state record. Students have been playing tennis at Highland Park High School since its opening in 1922.

Far left: *An HP tennis player eyes the ball going over the net in 2013.*

Left: *Members of the 1924 tennis team.*

Top: *Nancy Quinn and Shirley Martin, the 1950 girls doubles state champions.*

Above: *The 1924 girls tennis team.*

Above: Members of the 1964 girls tennis team.
Top: A Scot perfects his swing in 2008.
Top right: The 1953 boys tennis team.
Center right: Liza Graham Ellis returns a tough shot in 1989.
Right: A member of the tennis team practices in 2000.

Boys Track and Field

Highland Park has fielded a track team since at least 1925, and the early focus of the team was on two competitions: county and district meets. Many of the events from the 1920s are still around today, such as running events, discus throw, shot put, hurdles, pole vault and high jump. The boys track and field team captured its only UIL state championship during the 1939–40 school year. HP athletes have won 15 individual state track titles. The boys used to train at Highlander Stadium, but they now practice at Germany Park. Seventh- and eighth-grade boys can compete in track and field events for the Raiders, and each elementary school hosts an annual Field Day tournament with various events and competitions.

Right: A Scot clears the high jump in 1953.
Top: The track and field coach instructs his team in 1949.
Far right: The Scots pass the baton in 1953.

Far left: *Perfecting the pole vault in 1977.*
Left: *An HPMS student stretches out in the long jump.*
Bottom right: *The 1964 boys track and field team.*
Bottom left: *The Scots always clear the hurdles, as shown here in 1977.*

Girls Track and Field

The Lady Scots began UIL competition during the 1974–75 school year. The squad was made up of 18 girls, and they began the season by running in long-distance events. Today, many of the girls run for the cross country team in the fall before joining the track and field team in the spring. The girls compete in individual and relay running events as well as field events, such as discus throw, shot put, pole vault and long jump. The Lady Scots have won seven gold medals in individual events at the UIL State Championship meet.

Above: The 1924 girls track and field team.
Top right: The 1977 squad.
Bottom right: A Lady Scot soars in the high jump in 1987.

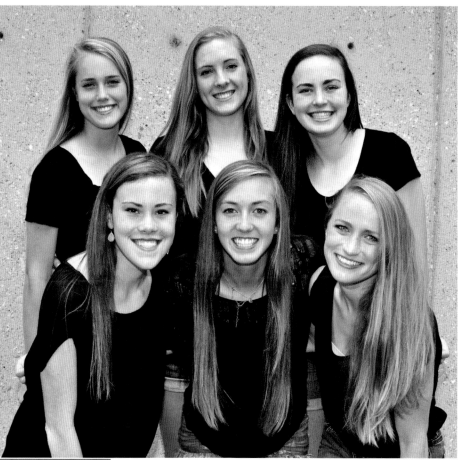

Left: *A Lady Scot shows off her hurdling skills in 1983.*

Far left: *A middle school athlete races for the finish line in 2014.*

Top left: *The HPMS track team in 1989.*

Top right: *The captains of the 2013–14 Lady Scots track and field team.*

Wrestling

Wrestling is one of the newer sports at HPHS, beginning during the 1982–83 school year. The team had 31 members its first year. In 1999, HP became the first school to win a UIL state tournament championship in wrestling. Overall, the program has won eight state team dual championships and five state UIL tournament team titles. Since the beginning of the program, 92 wrestlers have earned all-state medals, including 16 individual state champions.

Above: A Scot tries to throw his opponent in 2006.
Top: A Scot goes for the pin in 1983.
Right: A wrestling match in 2006.

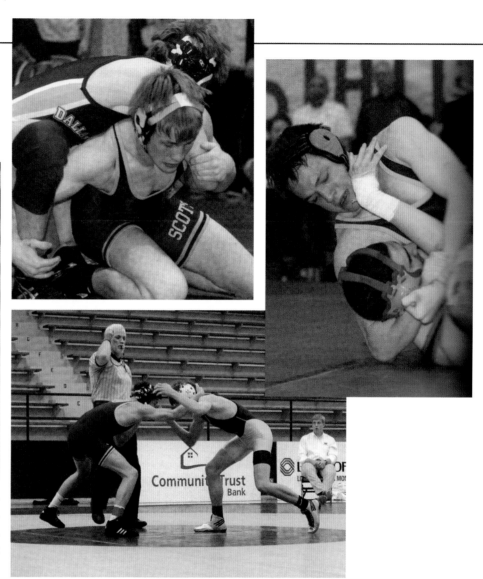

Above: *A Scot Slam in 2008.*
Top center: *A Scot relies on his endurance during a 2008 match.*
Top right: *An opponent experiences an HP headlock in 2008.*
Bottom center: *A 2013 wrestling match hosted at HP.*

Volleyball

The volleyball program at Highland Park High School originated during the 1925–26 school year. The inaugural team won the first county championship it entered, defeating Garland High School. For many years after that, girls played volleyball as an intramural sport until the first year of district play began in 1976. The Lady Scots have twice finished second in the UIL state championship, falling to Stephenville in 2003 and Hereford in 2008. The Lady Scots have won nine district championships, and have made 17 consecutive trips to the playoffs. From 2003 to 2013, the Lady Scots were ranked as one of the top 10 teams in the state. HPMS hosts seventh- and eighth-grade teams for its young Lady Raiders.

Above: *Girls practice their serves in 1966.*
Top: *HP won the county championship in 1927.*
Center: *The 1946 volleyball team.*
Bottom: *The Lady Scots in 1977.*

Above: *The 2013–14 Lady Scots volleyball team.*
Top left: *The Lady Scots set up a spike in 2008.*
Top right: *The Lady Raiders middle school team in 2008.*
Center right: *Varsity Coach Michael Dearman earned his 500th career win in 2013.*
Bottom right: *The Lady Scots go for a dig in 2013.*

YMCA

Before becoming full-fledged Scots, young Park Cities residents often get their first taste of competitive sports at the YMCA. The young athletes form into teams grouped by elementary school and grade, and they compete in flag football, tackle football, volleyball, basketball, cheerleading, baseball, softball, soccer and a spring track meet. Parents even get in on the action, helping train and coach the players.

Left: A girls YMCA team from Hyer, 1976.
Top: A Bradfield football team from 1975.
Above: The University Park football team in 1977.

Above: *A Park Cities YMCA soccer match in 1992.*
Top left: *Hyer girls stretch before a race in 1983.*
Top right: *Bradfield players huddle before a play in 1992.*
Bottom right: *YMCA friends from Hyer and Armstrong in 2004.*
Bottom center: *An Armstrong student is determined to make it to first base.*

Crew

A group of HPHS students formed HP Crew in 2002 and within two years began racing at the national level. The club soon welcomed rowers from all high schools in the Dallas area. The coed team is based at White Rock Lake and is now known as Dallas United Crew. The club travels across the country for regattas, including races in Atlanta, St. Louis, Cincinnati, Philadelphia and Austin.

Top: *HP rowers in 2006.*
Bottom right: *Carrying the load in 2006.*
Right: *Girls preparing for a competition in 2006.*

Above: Dallas United Crew in 2013.
Top left: A rower pulls with all her strength in 2006.
Top right: Teammates carry their boat after a competition in 2008.
Center right: HP gliding through the water in 2008.
Right: HP Crew during a 2008 regatta.

Boys Lacrosse

The HP boys lacrosse club team was formed in 1995 and is open to students who live within HPISD's boundaries. The first team was made up of 21 high school students, and the club has since exploded in popularity, now boasting more than 600 students and 61 teams across all age levels. The high school club team competes in the Texas High School Lacrosse League and has won six Division I state championships and two Division II state championships.

Far left: *Running after the ball in 2000.*
Left: *HP lacrosse in 2000.*
Top right: *Celebrating a win in 1999.*
Above: *A Scot caught in the middle during a match in 1999.*

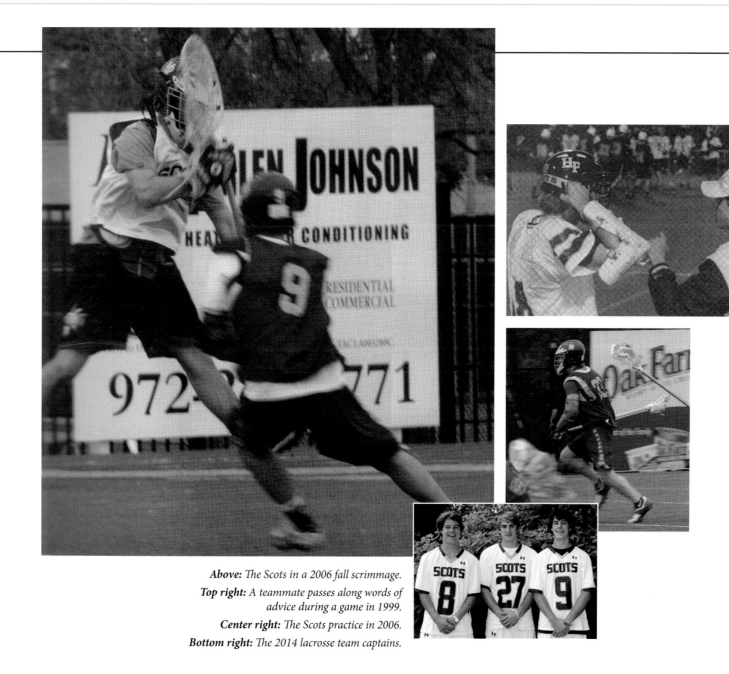

Above: The Scots in a 2006 fall scrimmage.
Top right: A teammate passes along words of advice during a game in 1999.
Center right: The Scots practice in 2006.
Bottom right: The 2014 lacrosse team captains.

Girls Lacrosse

The HP girls lacrosse team is a club sport open to all girls living within HPISD's boundaries. Girls in high school can compete for the varsity and JV teams, middle school students can join the seventh- and eighth-grade teams, and a second- through fourth-grade team is available for elementary students. This team sport is relatively new within the Park Cities but is quickly growing into a popular sport for young women.

Top: *The Lady Scots battle for the ball in 2006.*
Right: *The Lady Scots don their kilts for a game against Trinity Christian Academy in 2006.*

Left: *The Lady Scots practice their shooting skills in 2008.*
Top: *The Lady Scots lacrosse team in 2010.*
Right: *A Lady Scot looks to score.*
Center: *Passing to a teammate.*

Boys Hockey

The Highland Park Scots hockey club first hit the ice in the 1999–2000 school year. While the team is not a school-sponsored sport, the roster is heavily stacked with HPHS students. As the club's popularity expanded, a JV squad was added in 2001. Each year the Scots host an Alumni Game and invite former players back to lace up their skates and face the current group of students. The varsity squad has performed well, earning second place in the 2005 Texas State Cup and two second place finishes in the city championship.

Top: The Scots in a faceoff in 2000.
Right: HP vs. McKinney in 2008.

Left: *A Scot showing off his stick-handling skills in 2014.*
Top: *Celebrating after a win in 2012.*
Above: *Looking for a goal in 2014.*

Field Hockey

Field hockey is a relatively new club sport for girls attending HPHS, and the team is continually attracting new players. The season is brief but busy, running August through November. The HP field hockey team competes against private schools in the Metroplex, since no other public school has a team at this time.

Seniors from the 2013–14 field hockey team.

Left: The Lady Scots after a big win.
Center left: The HP field hockey team in 2013.
Top: The Lady Scots pose for a team photo.
Center right: Winding up for a big shot in 2013.
Center: Playing defense in 2013.

UIL Championships (Athletics)

TEAM	TEAM/INDIVIDUAL	YEAR
Boys Track and Field	Team	1939-40
Boys Track and Field - 440-yard dash	Larry Wolf	1939-40
Boys Track and Field - 880-yard run	Ralph Schrimpf	1939-40
Boys Track and Field - one mile relay	Relay team	1940-41
Football	Team	1945-46 (tie)
Tennis - Boys Singles	Dixon Osborne	1946-47
Tennis - Girls Doubles	Joan Aken / Carol Clabaugh	1946-47
Tennis - Boys Doubles	Wayne Bennett / Dan Stansberry	1948-49
Boys Golf	Team	1949-50
Boys Track and Field - pole vault	Dick Bernet	1949-50
Tennis - Boys Singles	Walton Miller	1949-50
Tennis - Girls Doubles	Nancy Quinn / Shirley Martin	1949-50
Boys Golf	Stewart Carrell	1950-51
Boys Golf	Team	1950-51
Tennis - Girls Singles	Jackie Johannes	1950-51
Tennis - Girls Singles	Jackie Johannes	1951-52
Tennis - Boys Singles	Eddie Sledge	1955-56
Football	Team	1957-58
Tennis - Girls Doubles	Jean Johannes / Jean Van Tassell	1957-58
Tennis - Girls Doubles	Jean Johannes / Jean Van Tassell	1958-59
Boys Track and Field - 180-yard low hurdles	John Roderick	1959-60
Boys Track and Field - 440-yard relay	Relay team	1959-60
Boys Track and Field - 180-yard low hurdles	John Roderick	1961-62
Tennis - Boys Singles	Cliff Richey	1962-63

TEAM	TEAM/INDIVIDUAL	YEAR
Boys Track and Field - 100-yard dash	George Aldredge	1963-64
Boys Track and Field - 220-yard dash	George Aldredge	1963-64
Tennis - Girls Singles	Betty Hagerman	1965-66
Boys Swimming - 100-yard butterfly	Paul Hayes	1969-70
Boys Swimming - 100-yard butterfly	Paul Hayes	1970-71
Boys Swimming - 400-yard freestyle relay	Relay team	1970-71
Girls Swimming - 400-yard freestyle relay	Relay team	1970-71
Boys Swimming - 100-yard butterfly	Paul Hayes	1971-72
Boys Swimming - 400-yard freestyle relay	Relay team	1971-72
Girls Swimming - 100-yard breaststroke	Sarah Sanford	1973-74
Boys Golf	Team	1976-77
Tennis - Boys Singles	Reed Freeman	1976-77
Tennis - Girls Doubles	Susie Low / Jan Johansen	1976-77
Tennis - Boys Doubles	Chris Doan / Talbot Davis	1977-78
Boys Swimming - 100-yard backstroke	Bruce Hayes	1980-81
Boys Swimming - 200 yard individual medley	Bruce Hayes	1980-81
Boys Swimming - 200-yard freestyle	Mike Heath	1980-81
Boys Swimming - 500-yard freestyle	Mike Heath	1980-81
Boys Swimming - 200-yard freestyle	Mike Heath	1981-82

Source: UIL centennial website – www.uil100.org

TEAM	TEAM/INDIVIDUAL	YEAR
Boys Swimming - 500-yard freestyle	Mike Heath	1981-82
Girls Cross Country	Team	1981-82
Boys Track and Field - long jump	Adam Cox	1982-83
Girls Cross Country	Team	1982-83
Girls Swimming - 100-yard freestyle	Katie Carson	1982-83
Girls Swimming - 200-yard freestyle	Katie Carson	1982-83
Girls Swimming - 100-yard freestyle	Katie Carson	1983-84
Girls Swimming - 200-yard freestyle	Katie Carson	1983-84
Girls Cross Country	Crystal McGuire	1984-85
Girls Track and Field - 3,200-meter run	Crystal McGuire	1984-85
Girls Track and Field - 3,200-meter run	Crystal McGuire	1985-86
Boys Swimming - 200-yard freestyle	Sal Vassalo	1986-87
Girls Swimming - 100-yard breaststroke	Catherine Marcus	1986-87
Tennis - Girls Singles	Claire Sessions	1987-88
Boys Golf	Team	1988-89
Girls Cross Country	Team	1988-89
Girls Track and Field - 1,600-meter run	Jennifer Lapp	1988-89
Girls Track and Field - 3,200-meter run	Jennifer Lapp	1988-89
Boys Golf	Team	1989-90
Boys Golf	Trip Kuehne	1989-90
Girls Cross Country	Team	1989-90

TEAM	TEAM/INDIVIDUAL	YEAR
Girls Track and Field - 3,200-meter run	Jennifer Lapp	1989-90
Team Tennis	Team	1989-90
Tennis - Boys Singles	Andrew Menter	1989-90
Tennis - Girls Doubles	Shelly Terry / Shay Evans	1989-90
Boys Golf	Team	1990-91
Boys Golf	Trip Kuehne	1990-91
Team Tennis	Team	1990-91
Boys Golf	Team	1991-92
Girls Golf	Kelli Kuehne	1991-92
Team Tennis	Team	1991-92
Tennis - Boys Doubles	Ben Pritchett / Clay Evans	1991-92
Boys Golf	Team	1992-93
Girls Cross Country	Team	1992-93
Girls Golf	Kelli Kuehne	1992-93
Girls Track and Field - 1,600-meter relay	Relay team	1992-93
Tennis - Boys Doubles	Clay Evans / Ben Pritchett	1992-93
Girls Golf	Kelli Kuehne	1993-94
Girls Soccer	Team	1993-94
Girls Golf	Kelli Kuehne	1994-95
Girls Soccer	Team	1995-96
Tennis - Boys Doubles	Grant Carona / Loic Lemener	1995-96
Girls Golf	McKenzie Gibson	1996-97
Tennis - Boys Doubles	Stephen Perkins / Josiah Daniel	1996-97
Baseball	Team	1997-98
Girls Cross Country	Team	1997-98
Girls Golf	Maiko Senda	1997-98
Girls Golf	Team	1997-98

UIL Championships (Athletics)

TEAM	TEAM/INDIVIDUAL	YEAR
Team Tennis	Team	1997-98
Tennis - Boys Doubles	Will Clinton / Hayden Hodges	1997-98
Tennis - Girls Doubles	Alison Bradley / Elly Motloch	1997-98
Tennis - Girls Singles	Kendall Kline	1997-98
Girls Cross Country	Emily Field	1998-99
Girls Cross Country	Team	1998-99
Girls Golf	Team	1998-99
Tennis - Boys Singles	Will Clinton	1998-99
Wrestling	Team	1998-99
Wrestling - 103 pounds	Jacob Francis	1998-99
Wrestling - 119 pounds	Joey Marzuola	1998-99
Wrestling - 215 pounds	Anthony Schlegal	1998-99
Boys Swimming	Team	1999-00
Boys Swimming - 100-yard backstroke	Tommy Sacco	1999-00
Boys Swimming - 100-yard breaststroke	Brian Stephens	1999-00
Boys Swimming - 200-yard individual medley	Brian Stephens	1999-00
Girls Cross Country	Team	1999-00
Girls Golf	Team	1999-00
Girls Soccer	Team	1999-00
Girls Swimming - 200-yard individual medley	Whitney Henderson	1999-00
Girls Swimming - 400-yard freestyle relay	Relay team	1999-00
Girls Swimming - 500-yard freestyle	Whitney Henderson	1999-00
Wrestling	Team	1999-00
Boys Golf	Team	2000-01

TEAM	TEAM/INDIVIDUAL	YEAR
Girls Golf	Brooke Shelton	2000-01
Girls Swimming	Team	2000-01
Girls Swimming - 100-yard backstroke	Jennifer Blackman	2000-01
Girls Swimming - 100-yard butterfly	Candace Blackman	2000-01
Girls Swimming - 200-yard freestyle	Candace Blackman	2000-01
Girls Swimming - 200-yard freestyle relay	Relay team	2000-01
Girls Swimming - 200-yard medley relay	Relay team	2000-01
Girls Swimming - 400-yard freestyle relay	Relay team	2000-01
Boys Golf	Team	2001-02
Boys Swimming - 100-yard backstroke	Tommy Sacco	2001-02
Boys Swimming - 200-yard freestyle	Tommy Sacco	2001-02
Boys Swimming - 400-yard freestyle relay	Relay team	2001-02
Girls Cross Country	Team	2001-02
Girls Soccer	Team	2001-02
Girls Swimming	Team	2001-02
Girls Swimming - 100-yard breaststroke	Brittany Sacco	2001-02
Girls Swimming - 100-yard butterfly	Candace Blackman	2001-02
Girls Swimming - 100-yard freestyle	Jennifer Blackman	2001-02
Girls Swimming - 200-yard freestyle relay	Relay team	2001-02

TEAM	TEAM/INDIVIDUAL	YEAR
Girls Swimming - 200-yard medley relay	Relay team	2001-02
Girls Swimming - 400-yard freestyle relay	Relay team	2001-02
Girls Swimming - 50-yard freestyle	Candace Blackman	2001-02
Team Tennis	Team	2001-02
Tennis - Girls Doubles	Paige Evans / Jessica Leitch	2001-02
Wrestling - 130 pounds	Keegan Mueller	2001-02
Boys Golf	Team	2002-03
Boys Swimming - 100-yard backstroke	Tommy Sacco	2002-03
Boys Track and Field - 1,600-meter run	Pete Janson	2002-03
Girls Cross Country	Team	2002-03
Girls Swimming	Team	2002-03
Girls Swimming - 100-yard breaststroke	Brittany Sacco	2002-03
Girls Swimming - 100-yard butterfly	Candace Blackman	2002-03
Girls Swimming - 100-yard freestyle	Jennifer Blackman	2002-03
Girls Swimming - 200-yard freestyle	Candace Blackman	2002-03
Girls Swimming - 200-yard freestyle relay	Relay team	2002-03
Girls Swimming - 200-yard medley relay	Relay team	2002-03
Girls Swimming - 400-yard freestyle relay	Relay team	2002-03
Girls Swimming - 50-yard freestyle	Jennifer Blackman	2002-03

TEAM	TEAM/INDIVIDUAL	YEAR
Tennis - Girls Doubles	Amy Bedell / Lauren Osborne	2002-03
Tennis - Girls Singles	Jessica Leitch	2002-03
Wrestling	Team	2002-03
Boys Golf	Charlie Holland	2003-04
Girls Swimming	Team	2003-04
Girls Swimming - 100-yard breaststroke	Brittany Sacco	2003-04
Girls Swimming - 100-yard butterfly	Candace Blackman	2003-04
Girls Swimming - 100-yard freestyle	Jennifer Blackman	2003-04
Girls Swimming - 200-yard freestyle	Candace Blackman	2003-04
Girls Swimming - 200-yard freestyle relay	Relay team	2003-04
Girls Swimming - 200-yard medley relay	Relay team	2003-04
Girls Swimming - 400-yard freestyle relay	Relay team	2003-04
Girls Swimming - 500-yard freestyle	Natalie Sacco	2003-04
Team Tennis	Team	2003-04
Tennis - Girls Singles	Lauren Osborne	2003-04
Wrestling - 125 pounds	Matthew Hobar	2003-04
Wrestling - 171 pounds	Keegan Mueller	2003-04
Boys Golf	Team	2004-05
Girls Cross Country	Team	2004-05
Girls Swimming	Team	2004-05
Girls Swimming - 100-yard breaststroke	Brittany Sacco	2004-05
Girls Swimming - 200-yard medley relay	Relay team	2004-05

UIL Championships (Athletics)

TEAM	TEAM/INDIVIDUAL	YEAR	TEAM	TEAM/INDIVIDUAL	YEAR
Team Tennis	Team	2004-05	Girls Swimming - 500-yard freestyle	Allison Arnold	2006-07
Tennis - Girls Doubles	Amy Bedell / Katelyn McKenzie	2004-05	Team Tennis	Team	2006-07
Wrestling	Team	2004-05	Tennis - Girls Doubles	Abby Stainback / Taylor Schreimann	2006-07
Wrestling - 130 pounds	Matthew Hobar	2004-05	Wrestling - 171 pounds	Kyle Anderson	2006-07
Wrestling - 180 pounds	Fred Rowsey	2004-05	Boys Golf	Cody Gribble	2007-08
Boys Golf	Team	2005-06	Boys Golf	Team	2007-08
Football	Team	2005-06	Boys Track and Field - 800-meter run	Patrick Todd	2007-08
Girls Golf	Lila Barton	2005-06	Girls Cross Country	Sara Sutherland	2007-08
Girls Swimming	Team	2005-06	Girls Golf	Team	2007-08
Girls Swimming - 100-yard butterfly	Natalie Sacco	2005-06	Girls Swimming	Team	2007-08
Girls Swimming - 200-yard individual medley	Natalie Sacco	2005-06	Girls Swimming - 200-yard freestyle	Allison Arnold	2007-08
Girls Swimming - 200-yard medley relay	Relay team	2005-06	Girls Swimming - 500-yard freestyle	Allison Arnold	2007-08
Girls Swimming - 400-yard freestyle relay	Relay team	2005-06	Tennis - Girls Doubles	Natalie Leitch / Abby Stainback	2007-08
Team Tennis	Team	2005-06	Boys Golf	Cody Gribble	2008-09
Tennis - Boys Doubles	Casey Powers / Max Stevens	2005-06	Girls Swimming	Team	2008-09
Tennis - Boys Singles	Eric Olson	2005-06	Girls Swimming - 200-yard freestyle	Allison Arnold	2008-09
Tennis - Girls Doubles	Natalie Leitch / Anna Stainback	2005-06	Girls Swimming - 200-yard medley relay	Relay team	2008-09
Tennis - Mixed Doubles	Charlie Dunn / Katelyn McKenzie	2005-06	Girls Swimming - 400-yard freestyle relay	Relay team	2008-09
Wrestling	Team	2005-06	Girls Swimming - 500-yard freestyle	Allison Arnold	2008-09
Wrestling - 180 pounds	Fred Rowsey	2005-06	Team Tennis	Team	2008-09
Boys Swimming - 200 yard individual medley	John Bannon	2006-07	Tennis - Girls Doubles	Kellye McDade / Abby Stainback	2008-09
Girls Swimming	Team	2006-07	Boys Golf	Team	2009-10
Girls Swimming - 200-yard freestyle	Allison Arnold	2006-07	Girls Swimming	Team	2009-10
Girls Swimming - 400-yard freestyle relay	Relay team	2006-07			

TEAM	TEAM/INDIVIDUAL	YEAR
Girls Swimming - 200-yard freestyle	Allison Arnold	2009-10
Girls Swimming - 400-yard freestyle relay	Relay team	2009-10
Girls Swimming - 500-yard freestyle	Allison Arnold	2009-10
Team Tennis	Team	2009-10
Tennis - Girls Doubles	Abby Stainback / Kristin Adams	2009-10
Girls Cross Country	Team	2010-11
Team Tennis	Team	2010-11
Tennis - Girls Doubles	Sarah Cannon / Alin Piranian	2010-11
Boys Golf	Scottie Scheffler	2011-12
Girls Cross Country	Team	2011-12
Girls Soccer	Team	2011-12
Girls Swimming	Team	2011-12
Girls Swimming - 200-yard freestyle relay	Relay team	2011-12
Girls Swimming - 200-yard medley relay	Relay team	2011-12
Girls Swimming - 400-yard freestyle relay	Relay team	2011-12
Team Tennis	Team	2011-12
Tennis - Mixed Doubles	Connor LaFavre / Margo Taylor	2011-12
Boys Golf	Scottie Scheffler	2012-13
Boys Golf	Team	2012-13
Girls Cross Country	Natalie Rathjen	2012-13
Girls Cross Country	Team	2012-13
Girls Swimming	Team	2012-13
Girls Swimming - 100-yard backstroke	Annelyse Tullier	2012-13

TEAM	TEAM/INDIVIDUAL	YEAR
Girls Swimming - 200-yard freestyle	Annelyse Tullier	2012-13
Girls Swimming - 200-yard freestyle relay	Relay team	2012-13
Girls Swimming - 200-yard medley relay	Relay team	2012-13
Girls Swimming - 50-yard freestyle	Kate Boyer	2012-13
Team Tennis	Team	2012-13
Tennis - Boys Doubles	Luke Stainback / Hunter Holman	2012-13
Tennis - Girls Doubles	Nan Porter / Chandler Carter	2012-13
Tennis - Girls Singles	Elizabeth Porter	2012-13
Tennis - Mixed Doubles	Connor LaFavre / Margo Taylor	2012-13
Wrestling - 152 pounds	Nick Reenan	2012-13
Boys Golf	Scottie Scheffler	2013-14
Girls Cross Country	Natalie Rathjen	2013-14
Girls Swimming - 100-yard freestyle	Kate Boyer	2013-14
Girls Swimming - 50-yard freestyle	Kate Boyer	2013-14
Girls Track and Field - 3,200-meter run	Natalie Rathjen	2013-14
Team Tennis	Team	2013-14
Tennis - Boys Doubles	Connor LaFavre / Hunter Holman	2013-14
Tennis - Girls Doubles	Margo Taylor / Elizabeth Porter	2013-14
Tennis - Girls Singles	Chandler Carter	2013-14
Tennis - Mixed Doubles	Elizabeth Tedford / Mac McCullough	2013-14
Wrestling - 145 pounds	Stephen Dieb	2013-14
Wrestling - 160 pounds	Connor Creek	2013-14

Texas High School Gymnastics Coaches Association State Championships

Division II

TEAM	INDIVIDUAL	YEAR
Mens Rings	Adam Forman	1984-85
Mens All-Around	Adam Forman	1984-85
Mens Floor	Peter Hegi	1988-89
Mens Rings	Peter Hegi	1988-89
Mens Floor	Peter Hegi	1989-90
Mens Rings	Peter Hegi	1989-90
Mens Parallel Bars	Peter Hegi	1989-90
Mens High Bar (tie)	Peter Hegi	1989-90
Mens All-Around	Peter Hegi	1989-90
Mens Rings	Peter Hegi	1990-91
Mens Parallel Bars	Peter Hegi	1990-91
Mens High Bar	Peter Hegi	1990-91
Mens All-Around	Peter Hegi	1990-91
Mens Rings	Peter Hegi	1991-92
Mens High Bar	Peter Hegi	1991-92
Mens All-Around	Peter Hegi	1991-92
Mens Pommels	Duncan Welch	1992-93
Mens Floor	Burton Rhodes	1994-95
Team	Team	1994-95

Division I

TEAM	INDIVIDUAL	YEAR
Womens Vault	Laurie Harris	1966-67
Womens Bars	Laurie Harris	1966-67
Womens Beam	Laurie Harris	1966-67
Womens All-Around	Laurie Harris	1966-67
Womens Vault	Laurie Harris	1967-68
Womens Beam	Laurie Harris	1967-68
Womens Floor	Laurie Harris	1967-68
Womens All-Around	Laurie Harris	1967-68
Mens Rings	Graham Cathy	1996-97
Mens Rings	Graham Cathy	1997-98
Mens All-Around	Graham Cathy	1997-98
Mens Floor	Todd Hyden	2005-06
Mens Rings (tie)	Todd Hyden	2005-06
Mens Floor	Meyer Williams	2010-11
Womens Beam	Arden Howell	2010-11
Mens Rings	Meyer Williams	2011-12
Mens Parallel Bars	Meyer Williams	2011-12
Womens Bars	Arielle Iola	2011-12
Womens Floor	Arielle Iola	2011-12
Womens All-Around	Arielle Iola	2011-12
Mens Floor	Meyer Williams	2012-13
Mens Pommels	Meyer Williams	2012-13
Mens Rings	Meyer Williams	2012-13
Mens Vault (tie)	Meyer Williams	2012-13
Mens Parallel Bars	Meyer Williams	2012-13
Mens High Bar	Meyer Williams	2012-13
Mens All-Around	Meyer Williams	2012-13
Womens Bars	Arielle Iola	2012-13
Womens Floor	Arielle Iola	2012-13
Womens All-Around	Arielle Iola	2012-13

Source: Texas High School Gymnastic Coaches Association website – www.thsgca.org

UIL Championships (Academics)

TEAM	TEAM/INDIVIDUAL	YEAR
Declamation	Angus Wayne	1930-31
Journalism	Martha Harland	1949-50
Journalism	Team	1949-50
Journalism	Carol Hall	1953-54
Journalism	Nancy Cotton	1957-58
Journalism	Team	1957-58
News Writing	Jere Stallcup	1969-70
Ready Writing	Genie Leftwich	1973-74
Ready Writing	Rob Swann	1977-78
Editorial Writing	Mike Grable	1987-88
News Writing	Catherine Wildenthal	1987-88
Science - top scorer chemistry	Drew Puckett	1989-90
Current Issues	Matthew Livingston, Christina Lefevre, Elliot McFadden	1991-92
Science	Team	1991-92
Science - top scorer biology	Liam McCoy	1991-92
Science - top scorer chemistry	William Pritchett	1991-92
Science - top scorer physics	William Pritchett	1991-92
Ready Writing	Brad Falconer	1992-93
Ready Writing	Evan Pollan	1993-94
Science - top scorer chemistry	Carlos Tamarit	1996-97
Science	Team	1997-98
Science - top scorer chemistry	Yaroslav Klichko	1997-98
Headline Writing	Matt Johnson	1998-99
Science	Team	1998-99
Feature Writing	Kirby Van Amburgh	1999-00

TEAM	TEAM/INDIVIDUAL	YEAR
Science - top scorer physics	Sergoy Timafeev	1999-00
News Writing	Amanda Luther	2000-01
Team Debate	Jesse Forrester / Andrea Read	2000-01
Feature Writing	Annie Wyman	2001-02
Science	Team	2005-06
Science	Team	2006-07
Science - top scorer biology	Megan Tang	2006-07
Science - top scorer overall	Tianen Li	2006-07
Science	Team	2007-08
Science - top scorer biology	Megan Tang	2007-08
Science	Team	2008-09
Science	Team	2009-10
Science - top scorer chemistry	Tianen Li	2009-10
Science - top scorer overall	Tianen Li	2009-10
Science - top scorer physics	Tianen Li	2009-10
Science	Team	2010-11
Science - top scorer biology	Alex Levine	2010-11
Science - top scorer overall	Alex Levine	2010-11
Science	Team	2011-12
Science - top scorer overall	Alex Levine	2011-12
Science - top scorer physics	Alex Levine	2011-12
Science	Team	2012-13
Science - top score overall	Arya McCarthy	2012-13
Science - top scorer physics	Arya McCarthy	2012-13
Number Sense	Team	2013-14

Source: UIL centennial website - www.uil100.org

Cheerleaders

The first cheerleading squad, known as the pep squad, dates back to 1925 at the high school, and it was made up of only three students: one female "cheerleader" and her two male "associates." Boys remained on the cheerleading squad until the late 1990s, but girls make up the current squad. The cheerleaders can be seen at athletic events and pep rallies, cheering on their beloved HP Scots. In 2013, the excitement of being a part of the cheerleading squad became a reality for HPHS students with special needs. The Sparkling Scots performed at many pep rallies and on the sideline with the varsity cheerleaders for several football games.

Top: The first cheerleading squad was formed in 1926.
Right: The 1941 cheerleaders.
Below: Showing their Hi Park pride in 1963.

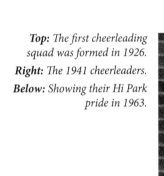

Left: *The Sparkling Scots rally the crowd during a 2013 football game.*

Center left: *The 1989 cheerleading squad.*

Top left: *Rah rah rah! A 1966 cheerleader.*

Top right: *Middle school cheerleaders in the 1970s.*

Center right: *High-flying stunts performed during a 2012 football game.*

Scotsmen

The Highland Park Scotsmen are an enthusiastic group of students committed to keeping the student body energized at football games and pep rallies. They can be spotted in their loud blue and gold uniforms, running across the field with flags that spell "HPHS" after a Scots touchdown. The Scotsmen also entertain the high school with their pep rally skits.

Top: A Scotsman encourages the crowd during a pep rally in 1999.
Right: Carrying the HP flag is an important duty for the Scotsmen.

Above: The Scotsmen looking tough in 1997.

Top left: Running the flags across the field after a football score in 2013.

Top right: The Scotsmen leading the team onto the field before a 2013 football game.

Bottom right: Scotsmen look for any way to show their Scot spirit — even with blue and gold pants.

Center: A Scotsman jokes during a pep rally.

Highland Belles

In 1983, an enthusiastic group of girls and a faculty member decided that something was missing from Highland Park: a drill team. After a tryout process and weeks of intense practice, the Highland Belles were introduced to the world at an inter-squad football scrimmage, where they promptly received a standing ovation from the crowd. The Belles debuted their trademark blue, gold and white fringe uniform the following year and quickly high-kicked their way into HP history.

Left: *A Belles Lieutenant performs in 2008.*
Top: *The Highland Belles debuted in 1983.*
Far right: *A Belle prepares before a performance in 1999.*
Center: *The Belles always cheer on their Scots.*

Above: *The Belles in Highlander Stadium in 2013.*

Top: *The Highland Belles before a football playoff game at AT&T Stadium in 2013.*

Center right: *The iconic fringe of the Highland Belles brings on applause during halftime.*

Bottom right: *The Belles have perfected their choreographed dance moves to create spectacular dance routines.*

Twirling

While the band plays during halftime of a Scots football game, you may see a baton fly high into the air, spinning end over end, only to be caught gracefully by a twirler on the field. This visual flair hasn't always been a part of the halftime performance. In 2005, nationally-ranked twirler Carly Bender became the first official twirler in Highland Park's history. She twirled for the Belles during her sophomore year and joined the band during her junior and senior years. Carly has passed the baton to a younger generation of HP girls who will carry on the tradition.

Right: Carly Bender, Class of 2008, was the first official baton twirler in HPHS's history.
Top right: *Amber Appel performing in 2012.*

Above: *Sisters Mallory and Amelia McMinn both twirled for HP in 2013.*
Top left: *Amber Appel standing at attention in 2012.*
Top center: *Carly Bender performs a routine with a blue and gold ribbon in 2006.*
Top right: *Mallory McMinn during a performance in 2013.*
Bottom right: *Carly Bender performs during a 2006 pep rally.*

Pipers

The familiar, rich tones of a bagpipe are present at many of HPISD's important events, including the Superintendent's Convocation and high school graduation. The original bagpipes were a gift from the Dads Club in 1934, and the pipers quickly became a symbol of Highland Park. The first group of pipers played next to the band during halftime at football games.

Top: The original bagpipes, gifted from the Dads Club in 1934.

Far right: *A member of the pipers performs the traditional Highland Fling in 1977.*

Right: *The bagpipers play before a softball game in 2014.*

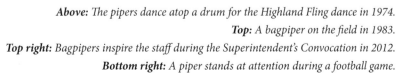

Above: *The pipers dance atop a drum for the Highland Fling dance in 1974.*
Top: *A bagpiper on the field in 1983.*
Top right: *Bagpipers inspire the staff during the Superintendent's Convocation in 2012.*
Bottom right: *A piper stands at attention during a football game.*

Band

The Highlander Band has performed at Highland Park High School since 1923. The band has played in the stands and on the field at halftime for HP football games and other scheduled marching contests. During concert season in the spring, the student musicians perform in individual, ensemble, and full band competitions. The band was formerly under the direction of the now defunct ROTC. Students in intermediate and middle schools practice their musical skills in the Raider Band.

Above: The ROTC Highlander Band in 1925.

Top: Middle school band members in 1963.

Center: The ROTC band practices a marching formation in 1953.

Bottom right: A band member waits to crash his cymbals in 1983.

Bottom left: A drum major leads the Highlander Band at a 1972 parade in Salado, Texas.

Above left: *A member of the 2003 middle school band performs during a concert.*

Above: *The 1991 band performs on the field.*

Top center: *Members of the 2008 Highlander Band.*

Top right: *Showing Scot pride in 2013.*

Center: *The Highlander Band performs during a 2013 playoff game.*

Bottom: *Highlander Band members make a colorful statement in their traditional plaid uniforms.*

Color Guard

The HPHS Color Guard, originally known as the Flag Corps, first made its appearance next to the Highlander Band in 1978. The Color Guard adds a visual flair to the band with choreographed dancing and spinning flags, rifles and sabers. During the spring semester, the Winter Guard performs and competes in indoor events.

Top: A member of the Color Guard performs a routine with the band in 1999.
Right: The Flag Corps sporting berets in 1983.

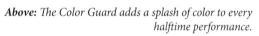

Above: The Color Guard adds a splash of color to every halftime performance.

Top left: A Color Guard routine in 2006.

Top right: Getting ready to spin a rifle in 2008.

Bottom right: Performing during halftime in 2014.

Orchestra

The Highlander Orchestra has performed since 1922, when the high school opened. The original orchestra included more than just string instruments and was made up of four violins, a clarinet and a piano. Today, the Highlander Orchestra performs with only strings and hosts several concerts each year, including the annual Halloween "Hauntcert" at NorthPark Center. The middle school also has an orchestra for interested seventh- and eighth-grade students.

Top: The first HPHS orchestra in 1924.
Center: The sixth-grade Armstrong orchestra after a performance in 1958.
Bottom: The Junior High School orchestra in the 1960s.

Top left: *A member of the 1983 HPHS orchestra.*
Top right: *Hitting all the right notes in 2012.*
Center: *A string quartet plays at the Dallas Country Club in 2013.*
Inset: *HPHS Orchestra Director Peggy Tucker and her musicians prepare to take a bow after playing at the Superintendent's Convocation in 2012.*
Bottom right: *A member of a string quartet playing during the Town of Highland Park's centennial celebration in 2013.*

Choir

Highland Park students have been singing for nearly a century, and the first mention of an organized group was the Choral Club in 1927. The Glee Club was added in 1930, followed by the A Capella Choir in 1947. The name was soon changed to the Lads and Lassies, and today they serve as the varsity choir group. The Lads and Lassies perform in many concerts at HPHS and in the community each school year. Younger students perform in the HPMS choral group and in the fourth- and fifth-grade honor choir. The honor choir is a voluntary group of about 70-100 eager students from MIS and the four elementary schools who perform at the annual Highlander Festival in the spring.

Top: *The HPHS choir in 1949.*
Bottom: *The 1964 Lads and Lassies in their choir robes.*

Above: *Ninth-graders in the 1967 middle school choir.*

Top: *The Armstrong School Choir prepares for a performance in 1965.*

Center right: *The Lads and Lassies serenade the staff with Christmas carols in 1982 in the HPHS library.*

Bottom: *Choir students are introduced to the choir program on the first day of school in 2011.*

Theater

Young thespians have been performing on the HP stage since at least 1920, when the Highland Park Dramatic Club was formed at John S. Armstrong School. In 1928, the club performed in a one-act play competition at McFarlin Auditorium at SMU, taking home the first-place prize. Today, the theater department at the high school performs four annual shows: the fall musical, the classic series, the senior play and the UIL one-act play. Students in the middle school showcase their acting abilities with annual plays and musicals.

Top: *The Dramatic Club on stage at HPHS in 1924.*
Center: *A Hyer fifth-grade Folklore Show from the early 70s.*
Bottom left: *A program of the 1962 HPHS performance of* Annie Get Your Gun.

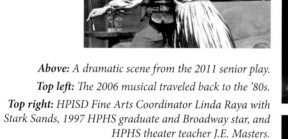

Above: *A dramatic scene from the 2011 senior play.*

Top left: *The 2006 musical traveled back to the '80s.*

Top right: *HPISD Fine Arts Coordinator Linda Raya with Stark Sands, 1997 HPHS graduate and Broadway star, and HPHS theater teacher J.E. Masters.*

Bottom right: *A program from the celebration of Linda Raya's 40 years in HPISD.*

Top center: *Under the sea with the cast of the 2013 middle school musical,* The Little Mermaid.

Bottom center: *On stage during the 2011 senior play.*

Media K–12

Today's students are growing up in an era in which media, photos, videos and information are shared at a rapid pace. Students use their technological talents inside and outside the classroom. At elementary schools, students write, direct and produce live morning announcements for their campuses, while students in the intermediate school host Skype sessions to discuss writing techniques with authors from around the world. At the middle school, a student-generated website showcases video coverage of news and events. The high school is always connected, as students use a TV studio to create new projects, update current events on the HPHS Media iPhone app and earn certification as computer programmers.

Left: *A Highland Park firefighter visited the Bradfield morning announcement studio to pick up Make-A-Wish letters in 2013.*

Center: *An HPHS student films a pep rally in 1974.*

Top right: *A student gives the signal for standby in the HPHS media studio in 2000.*

Top left: The UP KPAW television studio in 2013.

Top: Middle school students film in front of a green screen in their media classroom.

Center right: A student closes in on a tight shot for his video technology class in 2006.

Bottom right: A middle school reporter is live on the scene to cover Rachel's Challenge.

Center: A high school student looks through the lens in 2008.

Visual Arts

Young artists in HPISD have the opportunity to let their creativity shine from kindergarten to senior year. They express themselves through painting, drawing, photography, sculpture and multimedia works of art. Every spring, student artwork is selected from every grade and every campus to be displayed at the Highlander Festival. From there, many pieces of art go on to be admired on the walls of UP City Hall, UP and HP libraries, and the HPISD Administration building, where sculpture is also on display.

Above left: Students artwork adorns the halls at MIS/HPMS.
Above: Seniors show off their artwork during an HP Arts meeting.
Top: A middle school student begins her masterpiece in 2014.

Above: *HPHS student Blair Strong's painted cow was selected as a semifinalist in a national art contest in 2006.*

Top left: *Bradfield art teacher Jessica Smith helps her student finish her piece in 2013.*

Top center: *A Bradfield student works on a coloring project.*

Top right: *A budding artist in 2013.*

Center: *Students clip magazines to create collages in 2013.*

Bottom right: *Beth and Emily Felvey at the Highlander Festival Art Show in 2006.*

Right: *High school students share a laugh while putting the finishing touches on their artwork.*

Yearbook

The first yearbook, *The Highlander*, was produced during the 1916–17 school year at Armstrong School. There are no records of another yearbook being produced until the 1923–24 school year, the first year of the original high school. The book has been produced every year since and seems to grow each year; the 2012–13 edition of *The Highlander* boasted nearly 700 pages. The 1959–60 edition was the first to print a color picture, and in 2003 the entire school-year coverage section went full color. Students in middle school produce *The Legend* yearbook, and each elementary school publishes its own yearbook.

Above: The first edition of The Highlander *yearbook was produced in 1917 by Armstrong School students.*

Top right: The first yearbook staff in 1917.

Bottom right: High school students working together to produce the 1974 edition of The Highlander.

Above: *Flipping through proofs and spreads for the 2013 high school yearbook.*

Top right: *A student examines friends' signatures in his MIS/HPMS yearbook,* The Legend.

Right: *MIS/HPMS students and staff look through a year of memories in the 2013 yearbook.*

Newspaper

A group of HPHS students formed an editorial group in 1933, and soon thereafter the first pages of the student-run newspaper, *The Bagpipe*, were published. The paper has served as an outlet for students to report on current events at the school, athletic updates for the Scots, fashion tips and advice columns. Early editions of the paper even included relationship updates, where students could find out who was dating whom and those who were newly single. Today, *The Bagpipe* staff publishes six issues a year. Young journalists at the middle school write and produce *The Tribal Tribune*, which is also produced six times a year.

Top: The 1939 The Bagpipe *staff reviews the fruits of its labor.*

Center: High school newspaper staff members prepare to distribute copies of The Bagpipe *in 1955.*

Right: Carefully typing each letter for a 1969 issue of the newspaper.

Above: *A staff meeting in 1983.*
Top: *A high school reporter pores over her notes in 1977.*
Far right: *Students work side-by-side to finish the paper in 1991.*
Right: *From manual typesetting to online publishing, journalism students continue to adapt and report the news.*

Community Service

The motto of HPISD is etched in stone above the entrance to the high school: "Enter to learn. Go forth to serve." These inspirational words help set the goal of producing educated students with a passion for service. High school graduation requirements call for 50 hours of community service, yet a majority of students go above and beyond that mark. The average HPHS senior class completes 55,000–65,000 hours of community service time while in high school. The commitment to helping others begins at an early age, as students at all HPISD campuses participate in community service projects.

Top: Bradfield students show off gifts before sending them to Haiti in 1996.

Right: A student stands in front of gifts that were collected during a MIS/ HPMS holiday toy drive in 2012.

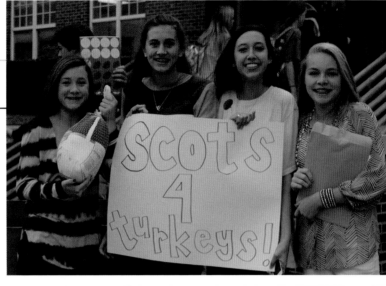

Above: The Community Service Council during a car wash in 2012–13.

Top: HPISD families donated more than 8,000 lbs. of turkey and nearly $11,000 in support of the North Texas Food Bank in 2013.

Center: MIS/HPMS hosted a bake sale in 2005 to raise money for the victims of Hurricane Katrina.

Far right: We need you . . . to donate a turkey.

Bottom: Students plant a tree during the Dallas County Day of Service in 2013.

Student Council

HPHS students were first elected to officer positions for the student body in the 1935–36 school year. This original Student Council became the governing body over activities and organizations for all students. The original council also appointed committees to help aid failing students, arranged all school assemblies and passed regulations concerning the election of cheerleaders. Today, the Student Council oversees the publication of the student directory, plans the homecoming dance, organizes a winter benefit and meets with campus administration and the superintendent once every six-week period.

Top: The HPHS Student Council in 1941.
Right: The HPHS Student Council in the auditorium in 1955.

Left: *2013–14 Student Council President Tanner Houghton speaks during the Superintendent's Convocation.*

Top left: *1976–77 Student Council President Mark Srere listens to suggestions from student representatives.*

Top: *The Junior High School Student Council in 1966.*

Right: *Student Council President Ed Mahon spurs on the crowd in 1995.*

Center: *McCulloch Middle School Student Council representatives in 1976–77.*

Hi-Lites

Hi-Lites was introduced to Highland Park High School in the 1930s as a service organization for girls and has shown no signs of slowing down. The 1931 yearbook describes the group's mission as the "promotion of various activities throughout the school and the furtherance of school spirit." Today, the all-girls group works with children in day care centers and raises money for the Make-A-Wish Foundation, granting one child a wish each year. Hi-Lites raises funds by hosting two dances each year.

Top: The first Hi-Lites group in 1931.
Right: Hi-Lites in 1955.

Left: *Members of the 1977 Hi-Lites.*
Top right: *The Hi-Lites in the 1971–72 school year.*
Above: *Hi-Lites hosted a pet adoption at HPHS in 2012–13.*

Literary Magazine

The Tartan is a literary magazine that was first published in 1952, but it did not reappear until 1965. The annual magazine features original poems, short stories and artwork created by HPHS students. A student committee must approve each piece before it is included in the magazine.

Top: *Staff members of* The Tartan *review submissions to the magazine.*
Center: The Tartan *staff in 1977.*
Bottom: *The cover of the 1985–86 edition of* The Tartan.

Left: *Artwork on the cover of the 2010* The Tartan.

Top left: *Students flip through the 2013 literary magazine.*

Top right: *The 2008 cover of* The Tartan.

Debate

HPHS students have participated in the debate program since at least 1923, when a team of boys and girls competed against other schools in the county. The Scots won that meet, and they have continued to perform well at local, state and national competitions. The 2004–05 team finished in second place at the National Public Policy Forum tournament at New York University. During the 2012–13 school year, the debate team won a state title in policy debate.

Top: Officers of the first HPHS Debate Club, in 1923–24.
Bottom: The Debate Club in 1937.

Left: *A student listens intently to his opponent in 2013.*
Top: *A recent photo of the HPHS Debate Club.*
Above: *A student drives the point home in 2013.*

H Awards

The H Award, also known as the Hall of Fame, is a special award given to Highland Park High School seniors and dates back to at least 1945. Originally, the award was given to top students involved in clubs and organizations, primarily members of the Student Council, *The Bagpipe* and *The Highlander*. The honor is still given today during the annual Senior Awards Day ceremony. The award is divided into four categories: Maximum Officers Awards, Gold H, Silver H and Bronze H. In addition to the previous organizations listed, awards are also given to members of the varsity cheerleading squad, the Highland Belles, the Highlander Band, HPTV and the Community Service Council. The awards are chosen by the sponsors of each organization.

SAM ADAMS
President Student Council
Maximum Officers' Award

Bottom left: The current H Awards, featuring the seal of the high school proudly displayed on top.

The Maximum Officers Award was presented to Sam Adams, above, and Mary Jo Goodearle, right, in 1945.

MARY JO GOODEARLE
Secretary Student Council
Maximum Officers' Award

The Hall of Fame
Highland Park High School during 1963-1964

MAXIMUM OFFICER'S AWARD

KATIE CHENOWETH — Business Manager of The Bagpipe
CAROLINE CHESTER — Co-Editor of The Highlander
LYNN FERGUSON — Co-Editor of The Highlander
PEGGY GRAY — Business Manager of The Highlander
JOANNE LEEDOM — Editor of The Bagpipe
CHRIS SLAUGHTER — President of the Student Council
SUSIE URQUHART — Secretary of the Student Council

GOLD H

FRANNY BONNEY — Bagpipe Business Staff
BARBARA BROCK — Highlander Business Staff
RITA GOSTIN — Publications Photography
LINDA GREER — Highlander Business Staff
LYNN LESTER — Highlander Editorial Staff
PEGGY MERRITT — Highlander Editorial Staff
NEAL STARKEY — Student Council
SUSIE STARNES — Bagpipe Editorial Staff
FRANCES WALKE — Bagpipe Editorial Staff
JOE TOM WOOD — Student Council

SILVER H

MYA COURSEY — Bagpipe Editorial Staff
VIRGIL HOOKS — Student Council
JENNIE MACKENZIE — Student Council
CHRIS MORGAN — Highlander Editorial Staff
KITTEN QUICK — Pep Rally Committee
HELEN REYNOLDS — Pep Rally Committee
ERIK RINNE — Pep Rally Committee
JAN ROTH — Bagpipe Editorial Staff
SUSIE STARNES — Pep Rally Committee

HONORABLE MENTION

JERRY ALEXANDER — Bagpipe Business Staff
BARBARA BRANUM — Highlander Editorial Staff
RONNY COLLINS — Bagpipe Business Staff
LEA COTTON — Bagpipe Editorial Staff
Student Council
MOBY DOWLER — Bagpipe Editorial Staff
BOBBY FREEMAN — Publications Photography
WAYNE HALEY — Highlander Editorial Staff
CINDY HENRY — Bagpipe Business Staff
ANNE HERRINGTON — Bagpipe Editorial Staff
JULIE HOOK — Bagpipe Editorial Staff
JIM LATIMER — Highlander Editorial Staff
NANCY MARTIN — Highlander Business Staff
BARBARA PUTNAM — Highlander Business Staff
ERIK RINNE — Student Council
JAY SCHWARTZ — Bagpipe Editorial Staff

HALL OF FAME

ALBERT ROBERTS
Bagpipe Staff
Gold H

MABEL WILHITE
Bagpipe Staff—Gold H
Highlander Staff—Gold H

Left: The Hall of Fame awards program from 1963–64.
Above: 1947 Gold H Award winners Albert Roberts and Mabel Wilhite.

Virgina Proctor, pictured here at 104 years old in 2014, shows off her HPHS yearbook photo from her senior year in 1927. Proctor eventually moved and settled in San Antonio.

Alumni

Alumni

There is no doubt that Scots go out into the world and make a difference. As noted in the first section of this book, Highland Park alumni have gone on to make their mark in every imaginable field. The list includes a Nobel Prize laureate, Academy Award winners, Tony and Grammy Award winners, Pulitzer Prize recipients, Olympic gold medalists, Rhodes scholars, a two-time Cy Young Award winner, a Heisman Trophy winner, Hall of Fame athletes, an astronaut, business and law leaders, entrepreneurs, scientists, doctors, artists, mayors, a governor and valedictorians of West Point and the Naval Academy who graduated in the same year. No doubt, the legacy will continue for centuries to come.

In this section, you will find more than 100 HP graduates who have received Distinguished Alumni Awards. You'll also find the Highland Park High School Alumni Association honorees for the Service Award (outstanding HPISD retirees) and the Highlander Award (people who have made a difference in the HPISD community).

This section also includes several spotlight articles about alums you may have heard about in addition to our Distinguished Alumni.

You'll also find pages dedicated to the military plaque at HPHS and the ROTC program that was such an important part of student life for many decades.

We all know couples who met as HP students and went on to spend a lifetime together. We asked several of them to share "then and now" photos. They are just a few of hundreds — maybe thousands — who found their lifelong sweethearts in the halls of HP schools. Many HP couples go on to raise their children here to grow up as Scots, and we asked several of our multigenerational families to send us their pictures to reflect that fine tradition.

Many thanks to the Highland Park Education Foundation and Alumni Association for sharing these unforgettable stories.

Dorothy Eloise Maloney

Class of 1941

Dorothy Maloney, a 1941 HPHS grad, began her acting career performing at SMU. She changed her name by dropping the "y," becoming Dorothy Malone, and in 1943 made her film debut in *The Falcon and the Co-Eds*. Malone performed in numerous films and TV productions, receiving an Academy Award for Best Supporting Actress in *Written on the Wind*.

In the 1960s, she took on the role of Constance MacKenzie in the television series *Peyton Place*. For that role, Malone received a Golden Apple Award, was nominated for a Golden Globe and received the Photoplay Award for Most Popular Female Star in 1965. She also has a star on the Hollywood Walk of Fame. In the 1992 film *Basic Instinct*, Malone played the friend of Sharon Stone's character.

Malone moved home to Dallas in the late 1960s to raise her two young daughters. She wanted them to have the same nurturing school experience that she had enjoyed in HPISD. Both daughters and her grandchildren have graduated from Highland Park High School — three generations flourishing in the same environment.

William J. McClanahan, 1927

McClanahan was a nationally renowned editorial and sports cartoonist. His work for The Dallas Morning News *covering Southwest Conference sports teams earned him a dozen National Freedom Foundation Awards. His work is greatly sought after by collectors, and many of his original cartoons are part of the permanent collection at the LBJ Presidential Library in Austin.*

Margaret Milam McDermott, 1929

McDermott is a patron of the arts and a philanthropist who has served on numerous boards in Dallas. She donated the first gift to the AT&T Performing Arts Center, and her contribution to the construction of the Meyerson Symphony Center helped move the project from an idea to reality. She was the first woman to be elected to the Board of Directors of the Republic Bank of Dallas.

Charles E. Seay, 1932

Seay was one of the country's experts in life insurance company investments. He was a well-known philanthropist who gave to local causes that benefited children, education, the arts and animal welfare. Seay made many significant gifts to his alma mater, the University of Texas, as well as to Scottish Rite Hospital, the YMCA and several Dallas arts organizations. Many buildings and programs bear his name.

ALUMNI

Fred Benners

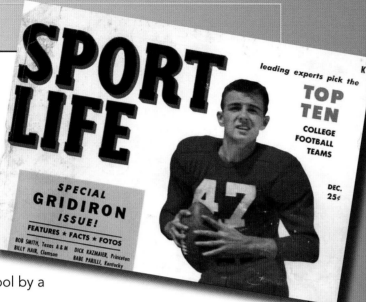

Class of 1947

As quarterback of the Highland Park Scot football team, Fred Benners led the Scots to the state finals in 1947, but HP lost to San Antonio's Brackenridge High School by a score of 22-13.

Benners went on to play at SMU, where he engineered one of the biggest comebacks in football history and is credited with changing the face of American football. As quarterback of the Mustangs in 1951, Benners and his team upset the mighty Notre Dame Fighting Irish by a score of 27-20. The game is remembered not for the score but for the 22 passes he completed and the 326 yards he gained in the victory.

Prior to that nationally televised game, the forward pass had been used in a very limited way as a surprise tactic and was not included in the game plan of any college teams. In this game, Benner relied openly and repeatedly on the forward pass to gain the yardage needed to beat the Irish. Immediately following that victory by SMU, teams began to utilize the pass as a key tool in their games.

After his highly successful career at SMU, Benners was drafted by the New York Giants. After playing a single year, he retired from football to pursue a career in law.

Gov. William P. Clements, Jr., 1934

Clements was elected the 42nd and 44th governor of Texas, serving his first term from 1979 to 1983 and his second term from 1987 to 1991. He was the first Republican to serve as governor since Reconstruction. In his later years, he was known for his philanthropic support of the History Department at SMU as well as UT Southwestern Medical School and many other programs. He was Highland Park High School's first All-American football player.

Henry C. Beck, Jr., 1934

A well-known builder with many of Dallas' highest-profile projects to his credit, Beck has served as trustee, director and chairman of numerous other businesses and educational and charitable organizations. As president of the Beck Group, he oversaw such projects as the building of the Cotton Bowl and NorthPark Center as well as Reunion Tower, the Hotel Crescent Court and the Hyatt Regency. In 2000, Beck was inducted into the Texas Business Hall of Fame.

Robert F. Ritchie, 1935

Ritchie combined a lifelong love of history with brilliant scholarship, devotion to community service and a distinguished career. He was an attorney whose avocation was studying the history of the State of Texas. He was active in many historical societies, such as the Sons of the American Revolution, Sons of Confederate Veterans and the Military Order of the Stars and Bars. He was an Eagle Scout, a Silver Beaver Award winner and served as a member of the SMU Board of Governors.

Maj. Gen. Andrew P. Rollins, Jr., 1935

General Rollins served in the U.S. Army Corps of Engineers for 33 years. He led engineer soldiers at home and abroad, in the Pacific Theater during World War II and in two tours in Vietnam. He commanded every size troop unit from platoon to brigade and was senior engineer on the Command Staff during his last tour in Vietnam. In addition, he served as post commander at Fort Leonard Wood. He was a deputy district engineer, a district engineer, Director of the Waterways Experiment Station, President of the Mississippi River Commission, Chief of Military Construction and Deputy Chief of the Corps of Engineers. Rollins supervised the building of NASA facilities and was appointed by President Nixon to oversee the construction of the Alaska Pipeline.

Rev. John F. Anderson, Jr., 1937

Anderson was one of America's most distinguished members of Presbyterian clergy. While leading Dallas' First Presbyterian Church, he was instrumental in starting its nationally renowned homeless ministry, The Stewpot, which is a resource for the homeless and at-risk citizens of Dallas. He was deeply involved in community affairs and spoke strongly against segregation.

George Underwood, 1937

Underwood is a respected builder, land and shopping center developer, and banker. He is credited with developing a segment of North Dallas and parts of Richardson and Carrollton. He also played an integral role in the planning and construction of DFW Airport. He served for 18 years on the SMU Board of Governors and the Board of Trustees. He and his late wife, Nancy, were major contributors to numerous causes across the city and were the lead donors of the Law Library at SMU, which now bears their name.

Pat Hudson Robertson, 1937

Robertson and her husband, Tex, fulfilled a lifelong dream when they opened Camp Longhorn in Burnet, Texas. She has been the camp mother to more than 90,000 children during her nearly 70 years there. Robertson's amazing ability to nurture each child's self-esteem and to make all campers feel welcome is illustrated by the motto "Everybody is somebody at Camp Longhorn."

Harvey Roberts "Bum" Bright, 1938

Bright's long business career includes oil and gas, banking and the trucking industry. From 1984 to 1989, he was owner of the Dallas Cowboys. He has also served on the boards of Texas A&M University, Children's Medical Center of Dallas, the State Fair of Texas, the YMCA and The Boy Scouts of America.

James M. Moroney, Jr., 1938

Moroney's vision, generosity and genial nature shaped The Dallas Morning News and its parent company, Belo Corporation, where he served as CEO. He was a farsighted business, civic and education leader who gave tirelessly to many causes both with his time and his talent. He was instrumental in the founding of Cistercian Preparatory School in Irving. He received numerous awards and honors during his lifetime, including the Pat Taggart Award for Texas Newspaper of the Year in 1987, the Theodore P. Beasley Distinguished YMCA Leadership Award and the Catholic Foundation McGill Award for outstanding contribution within the Catholic Community.

A. Starke Taylor, Jr., 1939

Taylor began his very successful business career working with his father at the Cotton Exchange. In 1973, President Richard Nixon appointed him to the U.S. Department of Agriculture Advisory Committee on Cotton. He was involved in open trade relations between the United States and China. Taylor was elected Mayor of the City of Dallas, serving from 1983 to 1987.

Don M. Houseman, 1940

Houseman is a leading Dallas insurance service provider and strong supporter of HPISD schools. During World War II, then First Lieutenant Houseman was injured and captured by the Germans at the Battle of the Bulge and held as a prisoner of war. He earned two Purple Hearts. Houseman demonstrated his talent for both leadership and service when he served as UP City Councilman from 1982 to 1986, followed by two years as mayor from 1986 to 1988.

Peter O'Donnell, Jr., 1941

O'Donnell is a well-known businessman who has actively contributed to the pursuit of excellence in education and medical research. Through his foundation, numerous gifts have been granted to the University of Texas at Austin and to numerous public schools in an effort to further his belief that education is the lifeblood of a great nation.

David G. Fox, 1941

Fox was known for his unselfish dedication to making his community and the world a better place. His fundraising efforts to keep the doors open at a South Dallas school and his leadership in raising $10 million for an endowment fund to keep seven other inner-city Catholic schools open are legendary. He is also well known for his home-building business, Fox and Jacobs, Inc. Fox also served as president of the Dallas County Historical Foundation and co-chaired the fundraising campaign for the Sixth Floor Museum.

Vera Jayne Palmer Peers

Class of 1950

Vera Jayne Peers, better known as Jayne Mansfield, graduated from HPHS in 1950.

While in high school, she studied violin, piano and viola along with French and Spanish. She performed in numerous school plays, always dreaming of being a star. She attended SMU briefly, transferred to the University of Texas-Austin and eventually to UCLA where she studied acting. While in college, she entered beauty pageants, winning numerous titles, including Miss Texas Tomato and Miss Bluebonnet of Austin.

Mansfield starred in many films and on Broadway, appearing with such famous actors as Cary Grant and Tony Randall. She starred in the films *The Girl Can't Help It* and *Too Hot to Handle*, among others. In 1956 and 1957, she received the Theatre World Award and a Golden Globe. One of Jayne's five children, Mariska Hargitay, followed in her mother's footsteps starring in the TV series *Law and Order Special Victims Unit*. Mansfield has a star on the Hollywood Walk of Fame. Her career and life were cut short when she was killed in a car accident in 1967 at the age of 34.

Ben H. Carpenter, 1941

Carpenter was a pioneering Dallas real estate developer, visionary and civic leader. He is best known as the creator, planner and developer of Las Colinas, one of the most successful real estate developments in the country. Together, he and his wife Betty have provided funding for scores of charitable organizations and causes.

Jane Manton Marshall, 1942

An accomplished and internationally known composer, performer and teacher of sacred music, Marshall has had a profound effect upon church music. Her anthems are carried by numerous publishers, and she has received lifetime achievement awards for her contribution to church music from the Southern Baptist Church Music Conference and the Fellowship of United Methodist Musicians and Worship Arts.

Dr. Elizabeth Gamble Miller, 1943

Dr. Miller is internationally renowned for her intellectual and scholarly achievements in the area of translation, making the depth and beauty of original Spanish writings available to the English-speaking world. She has spent much of her life as a specialist in translating the works of important poets and authors, such as the famous Salvadoran Hugo Lindo. Dr. Miller taught Spanish at SMU for more than 40 years and has served as Spanish Area Chair and director of the SMU-in-Spain program. She is also a respected and admired humanitarian, who has given generously of her time and talent in making annual trips to Honduras, translating for the physicians who perform surgeries on Hondurans in need.

Louis A. Beecherl, Jr., 1943

Beecherl followed a highly successful career in the oil business with decades of public service and philanthropy. He was twice elected chairman of the UT System Board of Regents, where he strived to make quality education accessible to students across the state. Helping others was the theme of his years of public service, and his passion was providing better health care and education for all.

Dr. Ted Votteler, 1944

Dr. Votteler was a pioneering pediatric surgeon at Children's Medical Center Dallas who, during his surgical career, separated seven sets of conjoined twins and performed more than 25,000 surgeries on children. He was named one of the "Best Doctors of America" from 1996 to 2000.

Robert "Bobby" Layne, 1944

Layne was an athletic legend who earned his way into the Pro Football Hall of Fame in 1967. He was the star quarterback at HPHS, where he and lifelong friend Doak Walker made a formidable duo. He went on to wow the Longhorns at the University of Texas, where he led the team to the 1946 Cotton Bowl Classic, practically single-handedly beating Missouri 40-27. Layne played for the Chicago Bears, New York Bulldogs, and in 1950, he and Walker were reunited on the field as teammates for the Detroit Lions. They led the team to the 1952 and 1953 NFL Championships. In 1958, Layne went on to play for the Pittsburgh Steelers. In addition to his other honors, Layne was inducted into the Texas Sports Hall of Fame in 1960, the Longhorn Hall of Honor in 1963 and the Cotton Bowl Hall of Fame in 2003.

Doak Walker, Jr., 1945

Walker was a football hero who won the highest honor in college football — the Heisman Trophy. During his career, he proved his versatility by playing running back, defensive back, kicker and punter, becoming a three-time All American at SMU and a four-time All Pro. He and Bobby Layne were lifelong friends, and with Walker at running back and Layne at quarterback, they were a tough pair to beat, both at HP and as teammates for the Detroit Lions, where they led the team to the 1952 and 1953 NFL Championships. Walker also played for the Boston Yanks. Walker was known and loved not only for his football prowess but also for his humility, and he was featured on the front page of many publications. The Doak Walker Award, recognizing the best college running back in the country, is named in his honor. Walker was inducted into the Pro Football Hall of Fame in 1986.

Elliot See, Jr., 1945

See was selected to be part of the second group of U.S. astronauts, one of only two civilians chosen for that role. He served as a backup crew member with Neil Armstrong on Gemini 5 and was selected as the commander of the Gemini 9 mission. Sadly, he was killed in plane crash prior to the mission.

Dick Bass, 1946

On April 30, 1985, at the age of 55, Bass became the oldest man to reach the summit of Mt. Everest, and he was the first person to climb the highest mountains on all seven continents. His challenges and accomplishments in mountain climbing are chronicled in his book Seven Summits. Bass was one of the original partners in the Vail Ski Resort in Colorado and has spent the last 40 years as the sole owner and operator of one of the premier ski areas in the country — Snowbird Ski Resort outside of Salt Lake City, Utah.

Jerry Fullinwider, 1946

In 1989, Fullinwider founded V-F Russia, and he was the first independent oil operator working in the USSR. He is known worldwide for his commitment to ethics in business practices. He is currently an advisor to the National Center for Policy Analysis and was a founding member of the Board of the Institute for Humane Studies at George Mason University. The Jerome M. Fullinwider Chair in Economic Freedom at the SMU Edwin L. Cox School of Business was named in his honor.

Jack Turpin, 1947

Turpin founded Hall-Mark Electronics Corporation, and he served as Chairman of the Board until its sale in 1993. Hall-Mark grew to become the third-largest electronics distributor in the world. He played a major role in the creation of five public tennis centers in Dallas, which helped make tennis available to the Dallas community and were a major influence in bringing the U. S. Davis Cup vs. Mexico tournament to Dallas. In 1967, he founded the T Bar M Ranch, the nation's largest Christian camping organization. More than 85,000 young people have benefited from the strong ethical and spiritual training they received at the ranch. Turpin was inducted into the Texas Sports Hall of Fame in 1989. He was President of the Board of Directors of the Dallas Theological Seminary from 1981 to 1993.

Lindalyn Bennett Adams, 1948

Adams is a community volunteer whose service to her city, state and country in the fields of health education, historic preservation and cultural arts has had a significant impact upon the city of Dallas. She earned such recognition as the Linz Award for the individual whose civic or humanitarian efforts created the greatest benefit for the City of Dallas and the Distinguished Alumni Award from SMU. She is perhaps best known for her 12-year effort in support of the Sixth Floor Museum at Dealey Plaza.

Dr. James W. Cronin, 1948

Dr. Cronin won the Nobel Prize in Physics in 1980 for his research on matter and antimatter, which led to the theory that the universe was formed by a "big bang" explosion billions of years ago. He went on to conduct additional experiments related to his landmark discovery and also conducted research in the fields of astrophysics and cosmic radiation.

David "Skippy" Browning, 1948

Skippy Browning was Texas State High School Diving Champion and a three-year All-American diver at the University of Texas. He won a gold medal in three-meter springboard diving at the Helsinki Olympics in 1952. The UT-Austin Swim Center diving pool is named in his honor.

James Cleo Thompson, Jr., 1948

Thompson was considered one of the most respected and successful independent oil and gas producers in the nation. He received numerous awards in the petroleum industry, including being named "Chief Roughneck" in 2001, the most coveted award from the Independent Petroleum Association of America.

John Nesbitt Leedom

Class of 1939

John Leedom graduated from Highland Park High School in 1939, and he is a graduate of what is now called Rice University in Houston. Leedom was an engineer, a political activist, a Texas State Senator, an author and a lobbyist. He was a member of the Dallas City Council for five years, chairing its committees on Finance, Public Safety and Cable Television. Leedom then served in the Texas State Senate representing the 16th district from 1981 to 1996. He is best known for sponsoring the law that established the Texas "Rainy Day Fund." While in Austin, he served on numerous Senate committees, including the Education Committee. After leaving the Senate in 1996, Leedom worked as a lobbyist seeking solutions for the water shortage in Texas. He wrote *Whose Water?* and *The Group and You* in response to Texas' water problems.

Charles Pistor, 1948

Pistor was an extraordinary family man, businessman and civic leader. He was greatly respected for his integrity, dignity, vision, generosity and faith. His banking career included serving as president of the American Bankers Association. He was honored by Financial World as one of the most distinguished CEOs in banking in the U.S. He served as a trustee and board member of many corporations and organizations, including the Salesmanship Club of Dallas, The Dallas Heritage Society, The Dallas Summer Musicals and the SMU Board of Trustees.

Dr. John Mathis, 1949

Dr. Mathis is an astrophysicist and professor of astronomy at the University of Wisconsin. Together with other astronomers, he provided analysis from the Hubble Space Telescope on the content of the dusty Magellanic cloud. His primary areas of research are extinction and interstellar dust.

Justice James A. Baker, 1949

Justice Baker, known as "Jaim" to his friends and classmates, built a long and prestigious record as an attorney and a judge for the Fifth District Court of Appeals. He was appointed to the State of Texas Supreme Court in 1995 by former Governor George W. Bush and served until 2002. His many publications on ethics in law are still used for continuing legal education. Justice Baker was loved and admired for his wit, wisdom and strong belief in ethical behavior in life, in the courtroom and in all that he did.

Leslie Ellen Melson and Clayton Edward Kershaw

Class of 2006

Ellen and Clayton Kershaw have already made a significant mark in the world. These high school sweethearts are both 2006 graduates of Highland Park High School. Clayton began his sports career playing Little League baseball before becoming the star pitcher for the HP Scots. In 2006, he posted a 13-0 win record and pitched an all-strikeout game in the playoffs, generating interest as an elite high school prospect. USA Today selected him as the 2006 "High School Baseball Player of the Year." Clayton was drafted by the Los Angeles Dodgers and debuted in the majors in May 2008 at the age of 20. He has twice received the Cy Young Award as the best pitcher in the National League.

After graduating from Highland Park, Ellen attended Texas A&M, earning her degree in communications in 2010. Prior to their marriage in December 2010, Ellen traveled several times to Africa to assist children in need in Zambia. Clayton also visited Zambia and fell in love with the children who meant so much to Ellen. Together, Ellen and Clayton launched Kershaw's Challenge to raise money to build an orphanage in that country. They have also authored a book together, *Arise*, to help bring attention and funds for the children in Zambia. Los Angeles and Dallas have also been beneficiaries of the Kershaws' volunteer spirit. Major League Baseball has recognized Clayton with the Roberto Clemente Award and the Branch Rickey Award for his humanitarian work.

In 2014, Clayton and Ellen headlined the inaugural luncheon and announced their support for Connecting Point, an organization devoted to creating an "all-inclusive safe, nurturing and stimulating day program" for adults with disabilities. The Kershaws are very special young alumni who are clearly committed to making this world a better place.

Pierce Allman, 1950

Allman began his career as a disc jockey for KGKO and was eventually promoted to manager of WFAA programming and production. As a young newscaster, he was the first on-site broadcaster to report the assassination of John F. Kennedy from the lobby of the Texas School Book Depository. Allman established his own marketing firm and coordinated many events in the Dallas area, including those for the Cotton Bowl Athletic Association and the opening of the Bob Hope Theater at SMU. He and his wife, Allie Beth, are the founders of Allie Beth Allman Real Estate Associates. Allman has been very involved in the community and has received numerous awards and honors. He was co-founder of the Park Cities Historical and Preservation Society and co-founder of La Fiesta de las Seis Banderas.

Dr. George E. Hurt, Jr., 1950

Dr. Hurt was a devoted physician who gave special care to all his patients, particularly children. He founded the Urology Clinic for spina bifida patients at Texas Scottish Rite Hospital and served as its director for 40 years. He received the Joan L. Venes Humanitarian Award for outstanding dedication and contribution to the welfare of people born with spina bifida. Dr. Hurt was also awarded the Dallas-Fort Worth Hospital Council's Distinguished Health Service Award.

William L. Hutchison, 1950

A successful oil and gas businessman, Hutchison has served on numerous boards and committees, including the Baylor University Medical Center and the SMU Board of Trustees. Hutchison and his wife, Patsy, established the Kimberly H. Courtwright and Joseph W. Summers Institute of Metabolic Disease at Baylor Medical Center, which is the first comprehensive facility dedicated to the diagnosis and treatment of children and adults affected by inherited metabolic disorders.

Donald Zale, 1951

Zale ran his family's jewelry business, turning it into a nationwide chain. When the business was sold, he devoted his time to opening the Zale Lipshy Hospital in Dallas. He has served as a member of the Board of Trustees of SMU and on the boards of many other educational and civic organizations.

Col. Warren R. "Bob" Lilly, 1951

Colonel Lilly was a much-decorated Air Force veteran who devoted more than 27 years to military service. As a helicopter pilot, he was shot down in Vietnam and held as a prisoner of war for more than seven years. Col. Lilly was a true hero and was awarded the Legion of Merit, the Air Force Commendation Medal, 26 Battle Stars and 18 Purple Hearts.

Dr. Charles H. Webb, Jr., 1951

Dr. Webb served as Dean of Indiana University's School of Music for 24 years. He was named a "Living Legend" of the State of Indiana by the Indiana Historical Society and was appointed by Secretary of State Colin Powell to the Committee to Advise the Secretary of State on Cultural Diplomacy.

Ed Bernet, 1951

Bernet was a standout football star at Highland Park High School and a second-round draft pick of the Pittsburgh Steelers. While in college, he and a group of friends formed a Dixieland jazz band called the Cell Block Seven. Upon returning from military service, he purchased a jazz club, which he named The Levee. His two bands, The Levee Singers and The Levee Dixieland Band, performed on television and in Las Vegas. In 1964, he established Ed Bernet Entertainment, a musical booking agency. In 2004, he was inducted into the Texas High School Football Hall of Fame.

Bob Coffee, 1951

Coffee is the founder and owner of an award-winning architectural firm in Austin that specializes in historic restoration and recreational projects. In 1995, he was elected to the American Institute of Architects' College of Fellows. He has served as president of the Austin AIA Chapter, the Texas Old Forts and Missions Restoration Association, the Austin Sculpture Center and the Texas Society of Sculptors. He established ranching interests in Texas and New Mexico and served seven years as a director of the Texas Longhorn Breeders of America and was voted "National Breeder of the Year." He is a well-known sculptor whose works include statues on display across the country, at the Zoo in Kabul, Afghanistan, the Dallas Crippled Children's Center and in UP's Coffee Park, where his bronze Waterin' the Work Mules *honors his late father, Roy Coffee.*

Art Barnes, 1951

The epitome of a servant leader, Barnes became the first president of the Highland Park High School Alumni Association. He was inducted into the North Texas Commercial Realtors Hall of Fame and won the Silver Anniversary Mustang Award from SMU. He is a past president of the Salesmanship Club of Dallas. He was a member of the HPISD Board of Trustees from 1972 to 1981 and led a number of committees for the district.

John Roach, 1951

Roach played football at HPHS and in college and was drafted by the Chicago Cardinals. After his military service, Roach returned to pro football as quarterback for the St. Louis Cardinals, setting the club record for most touchdown passes in a single season. He later became the back-up quarterback for the Green Bay Packers playing under legendary coach Vince Lombardi. He retired briefly, but was approached by Tom Landry in 1964 to come out of retirement and replace the Cowboy's injured quarterback, Don Meredith. After football, Roach began a successful career in mortgage banking. He became involved in the City of University Park and served as Mayor.

Megan Mylan

Class of 1988

And the Oscar goes to ... 1988 HP grad Megan Mylan!

Friends and family cheered with sheer delight in Dallas, Los Angeles and around the world Feb. 22, 2009, as Mylan walked onstage to accept the Academy Award for her documentary *Smile Pinki*, a story about a young girl from rural India whose life was changed after her cleft palate was repaired.

"As a storyteller, I look for compelling characters going through once-in-a-lifetime experiences. Pinki definitely had that," Mylan said. "I'm also attracted to stories of people making a positive impact in the world. I feel very strongly that this wonderful recognition is not just for my filmmaking but also a celebration of the incredible humanity of the people in the film."

HPISD Fine Arts Coordinator Linda Raya, who taught Mylan at HPHS, was not surprised that her former student had snagged the most prestigious film award in the world.

Raya remembers Mylan as a compassionate leader whose global vision was evident even as a high school student. Mylan was the president of Hi-Lites, a student activities organization that uses proceeds from its fundraisers to support local outreach programs.

Mylan also earned acclaim for an earlier documentary entitled *Lost Boys of Sudan*, which was nominated for two Emmys and earned an Independent Spirit Award.

Sylvia Ford Little, 1951

A successful oil and gas owner and operator, Little was the first woman president of the Independent Petroleum Association of New Mexico. She also served as a governor's appointee on the New Mexico Economic Development Commission. Little has received numerous awards for her service.

Peggy Nowlin Hanley, 1952

Hanley has dedicated her life to helping others. She was the first person to earn a degree in physical therapy from Baylor University. Her volunteer activities include the founding of the Junior Charity League, the SMU Campus Crusades Auxiliary, and with her husband, Don, establishing the Pine Cove Conference Center in East Texas and a mission center in the Fair Park area of Dallas. Hanley has made more than 30 trips to the Ukraine, Vietnam and Burma as part of Bible Education by Extension World, helping to train women leaders in godly principles.

Charles Robert "Bob" Palmer, 1952

Although Palmer was a student at Highland Park High School for only two years, his experiences have had a huge influence on his life. His favorite teacher, C.H. Marshall, helped him to realize both his ability and his interest in what would become his life's work, engineering. In 1972, he was named Chairman and CEO of Rowan Companies at the age of 37. Under his guidance, Rowan grew from a company of 900 employees with a value of $5 million to 5,000 employees and a value of $5 billion when he retired. Palmer is also known for his loyalty to his employees. During difficult times in the oil industry, he found ways to retain his employees, and in the process, positioned Rowan with grateful and well-trained staff when the industry recovered.

Dorothy Nettleton Masterson, 1952

Through her experience with the League of Women's Voters, Masterson came to understand the wretched conditions under which many Dallas families were living. In 1977, she founded the Dallas Tenants' Association, now known as the Dallas Housing Crisis Center, to assist families facing eviction. Masterson served as the volunteer Executive Director of the MADI Museum, the first permanent museum dedicated to the MADI art, which is distinguished by polygonal forms, contoured surfaces and geometric shapes. She has received numerous awards for her service to the community, including the Presidential Point of Light Award, the Lone Star Achievement Award from the Governor of Texas and the Women of Spirit Award from the National Jewish Congress.

Dr. Donald D. Clayton, 1953

Dr. Clayton is a nuclear physicist and an expert on principles of stellar evolution and nucleosynthesis. His primary research has been in the theoretical study of the origin of atomic nuclei in stars (nucleosynthesis) and the evolution of stars, the theoretical study of the occurrences of natural radioactivity and its implications, gamma ray astronomy, the interpretation of isotopic anomalies in samples from meteorites, condensation of carbon dust in supernovae and the origin of the solar system. His published works lay the foundation for five subfields of astrophysical research.

L. Lowry Mays, 1953

Mays is a public communications innovator and founder of Clear Channel Communications. His list of civic involvements is a long one, including serving as Chairman of the Board of Regents of Texas A&M University, as past chairman of The United Way of San Antonio and on the Board of Directors of Harvard Business School. He is a member of the Texas Business Hall of Fame and received the C.W. Conn Distinguished New Venture Leader Award. The Texas A & M School of Business is named in his honor.

Dr. Henry D. "Jake" Jacoby, 1953

Dr. Jacoby served as an applied economics professor at both Harvard and MIT and is currently the William F. Pounds Professor of Management Emeritus at the MIT Sloan School of Management. He is a former co-director of the MIT Joint Program on the Science and Policy of Global Change, which focuses on the integration of the natural and social sciences and analyzes policy as it relates to the threat of global climate change. He has a great love of music and has served his community in various capacities.

Mary Frances McClure Burleson, 1953

Burleson began her career working part-time as an assistant to Ebby Halliday. Today, she is president and CEO of Ebby Halliday Companies, the 12th-largest residential real estate company in the country. Under her leadership, the company reached a sales volume of approximately $5 billion annually and has become one of the most respected real estate companies in the world. She was named Realtor of the Year in Texas in 1999 and was the first Texan to be named to the Realtor PAC Hall of Fame in 2005. She served as a leader for the Texas Realtors Governmental Affairs Committee for more than 15 years and is a member of the National Association of Realtors Strategic Planning and Research Committee. Through her ongoing commitment to such groups as the Greater Dallas Chamber of Commerce, International Women's Forum, the Dallas Citizens Council and as a broker member of the Texas Real Estate Commission, she has helped make Dallas a better place to live, work and enjoy life.

James H. "Blackie" Holmes, III, 1953

Holmes has had a very distinguished law career. He was recognized as Texas Trial Lawyer of the Year in 2004, as a Texas Super Lawyer from 2003 to 2010, as a Distinguished Alumnus of the Dedman School of Law at SMU and as a Distinguished Alumnus of SMU in 2012. In 2013, he was named a Trial Legend by the Tort and Insurance Section of the Dallas Bar Association. He has served the community as a member of the University Park Community League, as Chairman of the Planning and Zoning Commission, as a University Park City Council member and as Mayor of the City of University Park for six years. During his tenure, a number of significant city enhancements were made or approved, including the renovation of City Hall, the construction of the Peek Center Emergency Operations Center and zoning for the George W. Bush Presidential Center. In recognition of his wise and even-handed leadership, the University Park Aquatic Center was named in his honor.

Shaun Jordan

Class of 1986

Shaun Jordan swam for HPHS' famed swim coach, Mike Sorrells. After graduating, Jordan attended the University of Texas at Austin, where he was a member of the team that won four consecutive NCAA championships. He was the 1991 NCAA champion in the 50-yard freestyle and 1989 and 1991 champion in the 100-yard freestyle, and held the 50-yard, 100-yard and 200-yard freestyle records for the Southwest Conference. He was captain of the swimming team at UT in 1990 and 1991.

Jordan won two Olympic gold medals in 1988 and 1992, and also won gold and silver medals at the 1991 Pan Pacific Swimming Championships. In 2012, he was inducted into the Texas Swimming and Diving Hall of Fame. He graduated from UT with a degree in economics in 1991 and an MBA in 1997 with a focus on marketing.

LTC Donald C. Bowman, 1953

After graduating from HPHS, Bowman attended the U.S. Military Academy at West Point, graduating in 1957 and receiving his commission as a second lieutenant in the infantry. He attended the Army Airborne and Ranger Schools. After qualification as both a paratrooper and a Ranger, he was assigned as platoon leader to the 504th Parachute Infantry Regiment of the 82nd Airborne Division. He spent his entire career working with elite infantry units. As a young officer, he chaired the Pathfinder Department of the Infantry School and developed the doctrine used by Pathfinders in the Vietnam War.

James A. Gibbs, 1953

In 1984, Gibbs founded Five States Energy Company, where he continues to serve as Chairman of the Board. He has been president of the American Association of Petroleum Geologists and is a Trustee of the AAPG Foundation. In 2008, he was presented with the prestigious Michel T. Halbouty Outstanding Leadership Award. He has been honored by the American Geological Institute with the William B. Heroy Outstanding Service Award and now serves on its Government Affairs Committee. He and his wife, Judy, served as co-chairs of the Tartan Endowment Campaign, raising funds in support of HPISD. The Library and Media Center at Highland Park High School has been named in honor of Gibbs and his family.

Stephanie Caroline March

Class of 1992

Stephanie March grew up in the Park Cities. After graduating from Highland Park High School in 1992, she continued her studies at Northwestern University, earning a bachelor's degree in Theater and Hispanic Studies.

She caught the acting bug while performing in high school productions under the direction of theater teacher Linda Raya. After moving to New York, March's acting performances have wowed audiences on the stage, on the silver screen and on television. She made her Broadway debut in *Death of a Salesman*. Later, she played a role in the film *Mr. and Mrs. Smith* with Brad Pitt and Angelina Jolie. She is perhaps best known for her role as Assistant District Attorney Alexandra Cabot on the NBC series *Law & Order: Special Victims Unit*. By coincidence, she attended HPHS at the same time as fellow actress Angie Harmon, who starred in the original *Law & Order* series.

She took on a new role in 2005 as the wife of celebrity chef Bobby Flay. Flay has several television shows on the Food Network in which March has appeared.

March is also a celebrity ambassador to World of Children Awards and a board member for Safe Horizon, an organization that provides support, prevents violence and promotes justice for victims of crime and abuse, and she is an advocate for women's rights. March has returned to Dallas for the HP Literary Arts Festival and for informal talks with students about her career journey.

George Reynolds, 1953

Reynolds was the founder of Reynolds Outdoor, a highly successful outdoor media and advertising company, but he is best known for his civic involvement. For decades, he has served the community in numerous leadership capacities — on the board of three banks, the Salesmanship Club of Dallas, as chairman of the Byron Nelson Golf Classic, as a member of the Cotton Bowl Association, the Church of the Incarnation's Foundation Board and as president of the Dallas Outdoor Association and the Outdoor Advertising Association of Texas. He was honored by his industry with the Dallas Advertising League's Bill D. Kress Memorial Award in 1982. He has chaired the Highland Park Community League, the Town of Highland Park's Adjustment and Planning Board and has served as a member of the Highland Park Town Council.

Dr. John Duckett, 1954

Prior to his death in 1997, Dr. Duckett was considered to be among the top pediatric urologists in the United States. Physicians and patients would come to him from as far away as Australia to seek his advice and counsel. He specialized in reconstructive surgical procedures.

Carol Hall, 1954

Hall is a well-known composer and lyricist for television, Broadway and off-Broadway. She has earned an Emmy Award, two Drama Desk Awards and a Grammy nomination. She received early recognition for writing the music for Sesame Street, and she wrote the lyrics and music for several musical productions, including The Best Little Whorehouse in Texas.

Gifford Touchstone, 1954

A successful businessman, Touchstone has devoted his life to serving his community through civic, charitable and educational activities. He has always had a special interest in the welfare of children. His service to the YMCA, Camp John Marc and the Salesmanship Club of Dallas has earned him numerous awards, including the 2005 Distinguished Service to Children Award. He served two terms as the mayor of the Town of Highland Park.

Wade Smith, 1954

Smith joined the firm now known as Touchstone, Bernays, Johnson, Beall and Smith in 1961. He rapidly moved from associate to partner to managing partner by the age of 39, a position he held for 25 years. In 1986, Smith was elected Town of Highland Park Councilman, and he served as mayor pro tem and as mayor. He has served the Park Cities Presbyterian Church as a deacon, Chairman of the Board of Deacons, Ruling Elder, Trustee and became Chairman of the Board of Trustees in 1999. He is a life member of the Salesmanship Club of Dallas and is on the Board of Visitors of the M.D. Anderson Cancer Center.

Maj. Gen. Charles Paddock Otstott, 1955

Major General Otstott graduated as valedictorian from the U.S. Military Academy at West Point the same year that Butch Thompson graduated as valedictorian from the U.S. Naval Academy. It was the first time two graduates from the same high school were ranked number one at the academies at the same time. They were recognized by President Dwight Eisenhower for their accomplishments. Maj. Gen. Otstott served in Vietnam, Europe and the U.S. and was awarded the Bronze Star Medal and Silver Star Medal. Both he and Thompson were also HP Blanket Award winners.

Sandra Jean Ford Fulton, 1955

Sandra Fulton has tirelessly given her time and talents to many organizations, both business and civic. She served on the Governor's Cabinet as Commissioner of the Tennessee Department of Tourist Development, and she has received numerous awards and honors, including being named one of the Most Influential Women in the National Travel Industry and the Tennessee Performing Arts Center's 1999 Applause Award.

Albert "Bud" Toole, 1955

Toole was the owner of a highly successful investment firm, which he sold to Compass Bank. Instead of retiring, he turned his attention to the founding of a Bible-based church in Jacksonville, Fla., which grew to more than 2,500 members. His missionary effort, East West Seminary, reached thousands of people living in persecution behind the Iron Curtain.

Lee Cullum, 1956

A well-known journalist, commentator and editor, Cullum has won numerous awards, including the Columbia DuPont Broadcast Journalism Award for KERA-TV, the public television station in Dallas. She has received honorary degrees from the Monterey Institute of International Studies and the University of Puget Sound, the Matrix Award from Women in Communications twice, the Woman of Achievement Award from Southern Methodist University and the C.E. Shuford Award for Outstanding Journalist in Dallas-Fort Worth. Cullum currently hosts KERA's weekly program entitled CEO, in which she interviews North Texas business leaders.

Alton K. "Butch" Thompson, 1956

Thompson graduated as valedictorian from the U.S. Naval Academy the same year that Charles Otstott graduated as valedictorian from the U.S. Military Academy at West Point. It was the first time two graduates from the same high school were ranked number one at the academies at same time. They were recognized by President Dwight Eisenhower for their accomplishments. Thompson has been highly decorated for his naval service. He served as commanding officer of the nation's first Trident-class nuclear submarine, the USS Ohio, and as commanding officer of the nuclear attack submarine, the USS Puffer. Both he and Otstott were also HP Blanket Award winners.

Ward L. Huey, Jr., 1956

Huey's tenure with Belo started in 1960 as a cameraman at WFAA-TV in Dallas/Fort Worth. He was head of broadcast operations for 25 years, followed by being named vice chairman of the board for 13 years prior to his retirement. In the broadcasting industry, he chaired the ABC Television Affiliates Board of Governors and the Television Operators Caucus Board of Directors and was inducted into the Broadcasting & Cable Hall of Fame. Huey served as an SMU trustee and as a member of the Board of the Meadows School of the Arts and the Maguire Center for Ethics. He is a past president of the Salesmanship Club of Dallas and has served as vice chairman of the Dallas Foundation and as a member of the board of Children's Medical Foundation of Texas.

Lynn C. Ashby, 1956

An accomplished journalist, Ashby has written for many publications, including The New York Times, The Dallas Morning News and The Houston Post, where he was a daily columnist and editorial page editor. His column continues to run weekly in The Park Cities News. He was named one of "Houston's Most Fascinating People" in 1998. He has served on the boards of numerous civic organizations.

Dr. Jack E. Little, 1956

Dr. Little joined Shell Oil in 1966 in Houston and rose through the ranks to become the president and CEO in 1998. Little has received awards for his business and civic endeavors, including the Texas A&M Distinguished Alumnus Award in 2000. He has devoted much of his time and talent to The United Way and The University Cancer Foundation at The M.D. Anderson Cancer Center in Houston.

Thomas E. Campbell, 1956

Campbell is a Vietnam veteran who served in the Marine Corps for more than 20 years. He served as White House Color Guard Commander under Presidents Lyndon Johnson and Richard Nixon. After his military service, he joined the faculty at the University of Texas in Austin and began his teaching career in the Department of Management. He authored numerous articles and a book called The Old Man's Trail.

Medora Doherty White, 1956

White gave tirelessly of her time and talents to many medical and philanthropic organizations during her lifetime. She was involved in the Junior League of Dallas, where she was named Sustainer of the Year in 1999, as board president and chair of the first fundraising luncheon for the Jewish Hospital in Denver, and as a life member of the board of the North Texas Arthritis Foundation and Trustee Emeritus of the National Arthritis Foundation. White battled rheumatoid arthritis but still found time to serve and recruit volunteers to assist in those causes important to her and her family.

Matthew Stafford

Class of 2006

Matthew Stafford led the Scots to a perfect 15-0 football season, winning the 2005 Texas 4A State Football Championship. After leaving HP, Stafford continued his football career at University of Georgia, where he passed for more than 7,000 yards and was named MVP in two bowl games. In 2008, he was named All-American.

He was the first overall pick in the 2009 NFL draft, starting his pro career with the Detroit Lions. Stafford was the first Lions rookie quarterback to start the season since 1968 and the third Scot to star on the Lions, joining Bobby Layne, 1944 graduate, and Doak Walker, 1945 graduate. Though it is early in his professional career, he holds a number of NFL and Lions franchise records. The 2013 football season ended with Stafford passing for more than 17,000 career yards, breaking Layne's team record of 15,710 yards.

G. Lee Griffin, 1956

Griffin began his career in banking as a management trainee in 1962 and became president and CEO of Louisiana Bank Shares, the first statewide bank holding company in Louisiana. He bought and merged banks in all of Louisiana's major communities into one large, strong bank. When hard times hit the banking industry and many banks failed, Griffin held his enterprise together and ultimately sold this institution to Bank One, now Chase. In August 2011, the Board of the LSU Foundation asked Lee to assume the full-time role of president and CEO of the Foundation. He joined the Board of Directors of the Foundation in 1981 and was named to the LSU Alumni Association Hall of Distinction in 1992. From 1997 to 2001, Griffin chaired the second half of the LSU Campaign, which exceeded its original goal of $150 million by more than 70 percent.

Jack Lowe, 1957

Lowe's career has centered around TDIndustries, where he has served as CEO and board chairman. Under his leadership, Fortune magazine voted TDIndustries one of the top five employers in the country. Lowe has also donated his time to ensure a better life for the children of Dallas by serving as president of the Dallas ISD Board of Trustees. He has received numerous awards and recognitions both professionally and personally, including the J. Erik Jonsson Ethics Award and an honorary Doctorate of Letters and Laws from Sterling College.

Barbara Lehde deRubertis, 1957

For 19 of her more than 30 years as a teacher, deRubertis provided inspiration to the Cashmere Washington Yale Elementary School, where under her guidance and leadership, the library became a model for other schools around the state and across the country. Her love of books coupled with her passion for teaching led deRubertis to become a distinguished author of nearly 50 children's books. Her series Animal Antics A to Z received the prestigious Teachers Choice Award in 2011. She is deeply involved in the cultural leadership of her Eastern Washington community and is on several boards and committees, including the Icicle Creek Music Center, Community Concert Association and the Charles Conway Children's Hospital Guild.

Peggy Pace Duckett, 1958

Duckett has worked in education, history and museums for more than 30 years. She served in both the Texas and Massachusetts Departments of Education and served for 13 years with the National Council on the Humanities. She planned, chaired and directed the Miracle at Philadelphia exhibition for the U.S. Constitutional Convention Bicentennial Celebration.

Michael M. Boone, 1959

Boone is a co-founder and member of the Board of Directors of the law firm Haynes and Boone. He has been selected as one of the 25 greatest Texas lawyers of the past quarter-century and the "Go-To-Lawyer" in Texas in the field of corporate/business law by Texas Lawyer Magazine. *He was also named the Best Lawyers' 2013 Compliance Lawyer of the Year, 2012 Dallas Corporate Governance Law Lawyer of the Year, one of the top corporate finance/mergers and acquisitions lawyers in Dallas by* D Magazine, *and one of the Top 10 Super Lawyers by* Texas Monthly *and* Law and Politics Magazine. *In addition to his highly successful law career, Boone is a passionate advocate for public education and for Highland Park ISD, where he served as School Board President.*

Stark Bunker Sands

Class of 1997

Stark Sands began his stage career at the age of 13 and, according to his grandmother, was in every play staged at Highland Park High School. He got a role from his first audition, during which he read from a cereal box.

During his years at HPHS, Sands also sang in Lads and Lassies and Park Version, the ensemble choirs that perform at events throughout the community.

Sands studied theater at the University of Southern California, appearing in more than a dozen plays and musicals.

His acting career immediately took off, as he landed a role on the HBO series *Six Feet Under* and went on to appear in several films. He returned to HBO to star in the miniseries *Generation Kill*.

Sands' singing and dancing talents match his gift for acting. On the stage, he starred in *Journey's End, Bonnie & Clyde, The Tempest, Twelfth Night* and *American Idiot*. In 2013, he made a splash as the star of *Kinky Boots*, for which he won a Grammy Award for Best Musical Theater Album and was nominated for a Tony Award for Best Actor in a Musical. That same year, he played a memorable cameo in the Coen brothers' film *Inside Llewyn Davis*.

Mike Sorrells, 1959

Sorrells is best known for his 33 years as Highland Park High School's swimming coach. He was a leader in the effort to separate the state meet into 5A and 4A and under divisions, which gave more athletes the opportunity to compete at the elite level. He was voted Texas Interschool Swim Coaches Association Coach of the Year in 2001. His teams won many state titles, the girls team in 2001 and 2002, and the boys team in 2000. He was inducted into the Texas Swimming and Diving Hall of Fame in 2012. He was also instrumental in starting the seniors swimming circuit, which provides higher level competitive opportunities for swimmers seeking national-level qualifying times.

Sam Burford, 1960

Burford has been an exemplary leader as an attorney and in his community. In 2006, he received the Justinian Award for his outstanding contribution to volunteer service. He served as mayor of the Town of Highland Park from 1986 to 1990 and was a member of numerous committees serving the town. He has served as Chair of the Finance Committee, on the Church Council at Highland Park United Methodist Church and as Chairman of Attorneys for The United Way of Dallas. One of his passions has been his longtime commitment to the Salesmanship Club of Dallas, where he was President from 1994 to 1995 and on the Board of Directors 10 times.

William T. Solomon, 1960

Solomon became president and CEO of Austin Industries in 1970, a position that he held until his retirement in 2008. During that time, Austin Industries grew to become one of the nation's leading commercial, industrial and infrastructure construction companies, as sales multiplied by a factor of 25 and grew to more than $3 billion. Solomon is an active and committed community member, and he has served as chairman of the Southwestern Medical Foundation, Hoblitzelle Foundation and as a member of the O'Donnell Foundation Board. He has received numerous honors, including the Linz Award, UT Southwestern's Sprague Community Service Award, the J. Erik Jonsson Ethics Award and the Dedman Lifetime Achievement Award for Philanthropy. He is also a member of the Texas Business Hall of Fame.

Richard Quick, 1961

Quick was one of the most respected swimming coaches in the world. At the collegiate level, he was named Southwest Conference Coach of the Year and was a four-time Pac-10 Coach of the Year. His teams won the NCAA Division I Women's Championships 15 times, and he was named NCAA Coach of the Year five times. He was the U.S. Olympic women's head coach in 1988, 1996 and 2000 and assistant coach three times. He coached at the Goodwill Games, World University Games and Pan American Games. Quick was inducted into the International Swimming Hall of Fame and was named American Swimming Coaches Association Coach of the Year four times.

Dr. William Howard Beasley III, 1964

Dr. Beasley earned a reputation as one of the country's most astute businessmen. He was adept at recognizing and seizing opportunities. After earning a Ph.D., Dr. Beasley became a special assistant to three Treasury Secretaries: John Connally, George Schultz and William Simon. He also served as the director of the Republican staff for the U.S. Senate Committee on Banking, Housing, and Urban Affairs. Upon leaving Washington, he returned to the business world and held several top executive jobs, including CEO of the highly successful Lone Star Steel.

Trisha Wilson, 1965

Trisha Wilson is a renowned interior designer and one of Dallas' most successful businesswomen. She is the founder of the Wilson Foundation, which has been instrumental in bringing modern education and medical care to South Africa's Limpopo province, an area with high levels of poverty and disease.

Kyle Rote, Jr., 1968

Rote was a soccer forward who played seven seasons in the North American Soccer League and earned five caps with the U. S. mens national soccer team between 1973 and 1975. He led the NASL in scoring in 1973. He later coached the Memphis Americans of the Major Indoor Soccer League, and he is a member of the National Soccer Hall of Fame.

Doug Wright, 1981

Wright is a prize-winning playwright whose stage work has been produced in cities around the world. In 1995, his play Quills *won an Obie Award. He went on to win a Pulitzer Prize for Drama and a Tony Award for Best Play along with numerous other awards for* I Am My Own Wife *in 2004. His career continued to boom, with nominations for Drama Desk and Outer Critics Circle awards for* Grey Gardens. *Wright always makes time to welcome his former teachers and their students to New York, and he returns to HPHS each year to talk with students to encourage them in the pursuit of their dreams of careers in the arts. Wright often expresses his appreciation to his HPHS theater teacher Linda Raya for her belief in him and her inspiration. He was the master of ceremonies for a tribute to Raya in 2013, during which the HPHS stage was named in her honor.*

Wendy Kopp, 1985

At the age of 21, Kopp founded Teach For America, a national corps of top-notch college graduates dedicated to teaching in underfunded and at-risk schools across the U.S. She has received numerous awards, including being named by Time *magazine as one of its 40 most promising leaders under 40 in 1994 and as one of its 100 most influential people in 2008.*

Lisabeth List, 1986

List gave up her hospital nursing career to join Doctors Without Borders. She works primarily in impoverished areas of Africa, East Asia and the Balkans. She has helped HIV/AIDS patients and has set up feeding centers and clinics in remote locations. In this role, she has offered help and healing to people suffering unimaginable pain and poverty.

The Kuehne Family of Golfers

Trip Kuehne, 1991 graduate; Hank Kuehne, 1994 graduate; and Kelli Kuehne, 1995 graduate.

Golf is in the blood of this Park Cities family. Hank Kuehne was a standout golfer at Highland Park High School, graduating in 1994. He attended Oklahoma State University before transferring to SMU where he was a three-time All-American. His accomplishments include winning the 1998 U.S. Amateur and playing in the 1999 Masters. He began his professional golf career in 1999.

Older brother Trip, Class of 1991 and captain of the Highland Park golf team, won back-to-back Texas high school golf championships. He was an All-American at Oklahoma State, won the 2007 U.S. Mid-Amateur and was in the 2008 Masters field. Trip was the 1994 U.S. Amateur runner-up to famed golfer Tiger Woods.

Younger sister Kelli, Class of 1995, was said to be one of the most promising women golfers to come out of Highland Park High School. She was a two-time U.S. Women's Amateur champion. While attending the University of Texas, she earned First-Team All-American honors and was later inducted into the Texas Sports Hall of Fame. She became a member of the LPGA in 1998. Kuehne was diagnosed with diabetes as a child and has been a role model for many young people affected by the disease.

All of the Kuehne children credit their father, Ernie, for giving them their start in golf.

Trip, Kelli and Hank Kuehne

SERVICE AWARD WINNERS

1989 — Ben Wiseman

Highland Park High School welcomed Ben Wiseman as its principal in 1928. He instituted many new programs during his 34-year tenure, including advanced math and English classes, a student counseling program, a language lab and diagnostic testing. In 1962, This Week magazine, which was included in Sunday newspapers across the country, recognized Wiseman as one of the leading educators in the U.S. after a study that was conducted recognizing schools with extremely high SAT and other test scores.

1990 — Martha Mary Stewart '34

Martha Mary Stewart joined HPISD as a junior high geography teacher in 1942. She devoted 42 years to making geography come alive for her students. She also found time to play the violin with the SMU Symphony Orchestra and was an active member of the YWCA, the Dallas Historical Society, the Freedoms Foundation and the Audubon Society.

1991 — Sara Ferguson Styring '42

Sara Styring joined the Bradfield faculty in 1950. In 1974, she became HPISD's elementary consultant and coordinated the special education program. She loved working with students with special needs, and her motto was "I choose to 'fast' from negative thinking and 'feast' on positive and productive thoughts."

1992 — Dr. Margaret Wasson

Dr. Wasson taught English and literature for 13 years at HPHS and served as HPISD's Director of Instruction for 26 years. Well-known in her field, she also published professional articles and held offices in numerous educational and civic organizations. Dr. Wasson received the Freedom of Valley Forge Award, Women of Achievement Award and the Delta Kappa Gamma Achievement Award for the Advancement of Women in Education. She also served as an official delegate for the American Association of University Women for conferences in London, Paris, Helsinki, Mexico City and Kyoto, Japan.

1993 — Walter M. Spradley

Walter Spradley served on the HPISD Board of Trustees from 1966 to 1984. During his tenure, he helped guide the district through a lawsuit that sought to consolidate HP schools with other area school districts. While he was a trustee, the district constructed a new football stadium, updated the campuses and introduced computers into classrooms. Spradley helped found the HP Education Foundation.

1994 — Dr. Winston C. Power, Jr.

After joining HPISD in 1966, Dr. Winston Power moved quickly from an administrative intern to assistant principal, principal and elementary/secondary consultant before being named superintendent in 1974. He was an innovator in a traditional setting who had a high-energy management style. He expected scholastic excellence and was instrumental in bringing the Academic Decathlon and Pentathlon to HPISD. He organized "Great Expectations," a national conference for principals of high-achieving schools to exchange ideas and discuss innovative programs.

1995 — Frank Monroe

Frank Monroe was a hands-on administrator who served for 20 years as superintendent of HPISD. He believed in providing excellent educational leadership and expected greatness from all students. Monroe was also active in the Park Cities community, serving in leadership roles in the Rotary Club, his church and the Dallas Society for Crippled Children. He brought a wonderful tradition to HP when he started the "Victory Apple" ceremony during pep rallies at the high school, a tradition that continues to this day. Monroe was awarded numerous outstanding service awards from educational associations and was appointed by Gov. Bill Clements to serve as trustee of the Texas Teachers Retirement System.

1996 — Edith Harris, '36

Edith Harris devoted 44 years to teaching history at HP Junior High and McCulloch Middle School, where she impacted the lives of generations of Park Cities students and families. Harris always stressed to her pupils that they needed to care for those less fortunate than themselves. In 1973, she received the Valley Forge Freedom Foundation Teachers Medal and was named Teacher of the Year in 1976.

1997 — Frank Bevers

Bevers joined HPISD in April 1974 as a high school physical education teacher and head football coach. After 10 years, he retired from coaching and served first as athletic coordinator for students in grades 9-12 and then as director of maintenance. He returned to coach the Scots from 1989 to 1992. With 134 wins over 13 years, he became HPISD's winningest football coach until Randy Allen broke that record in 2011. He was inducted into the Texas High School Football Hall of Fame in 2001.

1998 — Dr. E.A. Sigler, Jr.

Dr. Sigler joined the staff at Highland Park Junior High School as a teacher and coach in 1954. He later taught chemistry and coached basketball at Highland Park High School and was promoted to assistant principal. He was appointed principal of HPHS in 1973 and served in that capacity until 1982. Dr. Sigler was named to a group of outstanding principals by the National Association of Secondary School Principals, and the Southwestern Region of The College Board named him one of the top four administrators in a five-state region.

1999 — Walter Cecil Holmes, Jr. '55

Holmes returned to Highland Park High School in 1966 to teach world history. He went on to coach junior varsity football, varsity baseball, freshman football, and track. He also served as Student Council sponsor. In 1984, he was named attendance coordinator at Highland Park High School. In 1987, Park Cities People named him Father of the Year. Holmes retired in 1995.

2000 — Floyd R. Hightower

Floyd Hightower moved to Dallas in 1936 and became an assistant football coach and head track coach at Highland Park High School. He is best known for his success as a track coach. During his 18 years at Highland Park, his track teams won one state title, two second-place state titles, 15 regional titles and 17 district titles. His commitment to his teams was legendary. He was a mentor and role model to hundreds of high school students. After leaving Highland Park, he coached track at SMU.

2001 — Newton L. Manning

Newton Manning joined the district in 1940 as the first vice principal of the junior high and was later named the first principal at the new Hyer Elementary School, a position he held for 25 years. He turned the Hyer courtyard into a small farm with vegetables gardens, a goat and chickens to teach children about nutrition. After learning about dyslexia, a newly diagnosed learning difficulty, Mr. Manning brought in specialists to educate his teachers about this little-understood learning difference.

2002 — Kellis White

Coach White taught physical education and coached football and basketball at the Highland Park Junior High School from 1961 to 1992. White had a gift for guiding his students and players as they developed foundations of character, morality, self-respect and spirituality. In the early 1960s, White and Coach Albert Dudley petitioned the Fellowship of Christian Athletes national organization to get a charter for Highland Park Junior High School. They were turned down because charters were only given to high schools. The FCA finally relented and allowed the junior high to receive a charter. It was an experiment for the FCA, and the young HPJH club (known as a huddle) flourished. The group was hugely successful, and today the FCA has groups in more than 1,000 middle schools across the country. Coach White's ability to connect with and inspire his students left a lasting impression on them. In fact, HPHS graduate Kirk Dooley and his wife, Charlotte, paid tribute to Coach White by naming their son Kellis.

2003 — Dr. Kenneth Thomas

Dr. Thomas joined HPISD in 1978 as the principal at Armstrong Elementary. The community was inspired by his zeal, his innovations, his problem-solving ability and his gift for remembering the name of every student in the school. Dr. Thomas also served on mission trips to Cuba, Russia and China. After his retirement in 1995, he became a professor at Dallas Baptist University, and he continues to serve as a leading force in the Highland Park Retired Teachers organization.

2004 — Elaine S. Prude

Elaine Prude began her career in HPISD as a second-grade teacher at UP Elementary School in 1970, and she became principal at Bradfield Elementary in 1982. Prude was invited to the White House when Bradfield was awarded the title of a Blue Ribbon School. After retiring, she continued to serve her community by volunteering with the Susan Komen Race for the Cure, Meals on Wheels and the Byron Nelson Golf Classic.

2005 — Frank Story

Frank Story served HPISD as a teacher and substitute for 57 years, into his 90s. He was known for riding his bicycle to and from school each day even when he reached the age of 90. He was affectionately known as the "Mr. Chips" of HP. During World War II, Story was an interpreter in both Spanish and French, which gave him a heightened level of competence and appreciation for diverse cultures. He was a man who loved his profession, adored his students and freely gave the gift of his time to all who needed him.

2006 — Dr. Rodney Pirtle

In 1973, Dr. Pirtle left Ohio State University to become assistant principal at Highland Park High School. After two years, he became principal at University Park Elementary, where he remained for 10 years. His next appointment was as Director of Special Programs, followed by Special Assistant to the Superintendent. After his retirement, Dr. Pirtle and his wife, Beth, became involved with musical entertainment.

2007 — Mary Dillard

Mary Dillard's career with HPISD spanned nearly 50 years. As an English teacher at HPHS, she always saw more potential in her students than the students saw in themselves. Dillard was named Teacher of the Year twice and was voted Favorite Teacher in a senior student poll. She served as English Dept. Chair, sponsor for the National Honor Society, sponsor for UIL Academic Teams and the Academic Decathlon and assisted The College Board as an AP English Consultant.

2008 — Bo Snowden

Coach Snowden dedicated more than 30 years to HPISD before retiring in 1996. He served as a history teacher, a JV football and basketball coach, a varsity basketball coach and as HPISD's Director of Athletics. Believing that his role included being a supportive mentor, Snowden was known for attending every athletic event for both boys and girls. He was a consummate professional and a shining example of humility and integrity.

2009 — Becky Nugent

A woman of many talents, Nugent served as HPISD Director of Community Relations for 18 years. She played a key role in the founding and organization of the Highland Park High School Alumni Association. The Scots Illustrated sports program magazine was Becky's brainchild and has been a fixture for HP sports since its inception. After leaving HP, she became the communications and marketing director for the City of College Station. Her work has garnered her more than 350 state, regional and national awards.

2010 — Wanda Spoonmore

Wanda Spoonmore joined the faculty of Highland Park Junior High as a math teacher in 1958 and remained with the district for 36 years. Spoonmore served as the chair of the middle school math department and spent many hours preparing students for local and state math competitions. She has a passion for music, which led her to organize a singing group called the Clef Dwellers and an orchestra of district faculty members called the Notable Notes. After retiring from Highland Park, Spoonmore joined DeVry University as an adjunct professor and was named Teacher of the Year in 2004.

2011 — Shirley Kochman, '53

Shirley Kochman shared her passion for music when she joined the faculty of Hyer Elementary as music teacher. Her academic focus shifted as she became the first sixth-grade counselor at McCulloch Middle School and the first Highland Park ISD counselor who was trained in special education. Her love of music continued as she became a founding member of the Richardson Symphony Orchestra and also a founding member of the City of Allen Philharmonic Orchestra. She was recognized in "Who's Who" among Human Services Professionals and has received the Delta Kappa Gamma service award. Kochman distinguished herself as an outstanding teacher and counselor for more than 32 years.

2012 — Dr. John P. Connolly

In 1990, HPISD was facing new challenges, including rapid enrollment growth and new property tax recapture legislation. Dr. Connolly joined HPISD as superintendent and worked tirelessly to improve the financing of Texas public schools by forming the Texas School Coalition. Through his leadership, many district improvements and long-range planning initiatives were developed to strengthen the district.

2013 — Dr. Linda Salinas

For more than 25 years, Linda Salinas exemplified service to HPISD. She served in many roles — educational diagnostician, principal, and administrator. Salinas joined the HP family as a learning disabilities resource diagnostician in 1978 after teaching high school English and government and serving as a learning disabilities resource teacher in the Aldine district in West Texas. In 1993, she became the interim principal of Highland Park High School and was named principal of the Highland Park Middle School in 1994. She served as HPISD's director of personnel from 1996 until her retirement in 2003.

2014 — Dr. David Smith

Dr. David Smith is a noted author, public speaker and historian. He frequently addresses groups and conferences about the Civil War and publishes a blog about current events that puts them in historical perspective. Above all, however, Dr. Smith is known and honored for his passion for history, teaching and commitment to his students. During his time at HPHS, he taught U.S. History, AP European History, AP Government and eighth-grade social studies and history. For several summers, groups of lucky students accompanied him on a trip to visit several historic sites in Europe. Upon his retirement, a group of students and their parents paid a special tribute to David Smith by establishing a scholarship to honor the special impact he made on his students.

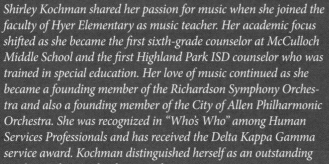

HIGHLANDER AWARD WINNERS

2004 — James T. "Brad" Bradley

Brad Bradley and his camera are fixtures in the Park Cities. Bradley is the smiling, warm person everyone has come to expect at all games and events in Highland Park, and he has touched the lives of many generations of Scots through his photography. Bradley is well known across the country for his sports photography, and he has been the official photographer for the Dallas Cowboys, Green Bay Packers and Chicago Bears. He is credited with inventing the TV color slide, a news broadcast term for when a photograph of a player being discussed appears behind the sports anchor. Perhaps even more than his creative ability, Bradley is respected and loved for his kindness and humility. He was the first recipient of the Highlander Award.

2005— Barbara Lomax Hitzelberger-Wooten

Barbara Hitzelberger-Wooten has dedicated her life to making the Park Cities a great place to live and raise children. Her service to the community began when her three sons enrolled in HPISD and included serving as president of the Highland Park Junior High PTA. Her citywide involvement grew in 1984 when she was appointed to the University Park Planning and Zoning Commission. From there, she served on numerous boards and committees before becoming the first woman to be elected to the University Park City Council and the first woman to be elected mayor in 1992. She has also served as president of the Highland Park Education Foundation Board of Directors, grand marshal of the Fourth of July parade and as honorary chair of the Dallas Museum of Natural History annual benefit. She was also elected to the Board of Directors of the SMU Alumni Association.

2006— Margo Goodwin

HPISD has benefited greatly from the hard work and hundreds of volunteer hours that Margo Goodwin has contributed. She has tirelessly served in numerous capacities, including president of the Highland Park High School PTA. Goodwin was instrumental in the success of the Highland Park Education Foundation, serving as president, secretary and treasurer of the Board of Directors as well as heading the annual fundraising campaign. She was a co-chair of the first combined Mad for Plaid annual giving campaign. She has also been involved in the Junior League and was named Sustainer of the Year in 2003. She serves on the Baylor Health Care System Foundation Board of Directors, the Board of Dallas CASA, as a Byron Nelson Tournament volunteer and as Ball Chairman of the 2004 Crystal Charity Ball.

2007 — Kirk Dooley, '73

Dooley has always been a leader in the Park Cities community as a coach, volunteer and parent. For several years, he taught Leadership 101 for students at HPHS, an extracurricular class taught in the evening for selected team and school leaders, and he continues to speak at the Freshman Leadership Class each year. For more than 15 years, he and his wife, Charlotte, have published the Scots Illustrated program for HP sports. Dooley is lovingly known as the trash man, constantly walking the campuses and picking up after others to help keep the areas beautiful. All the while, he still finds time to write his weekly column for The Dallas Morning News.

2008 — Dr. David Webb, '51

In 1964, young Dr. Webb was invited to a Friday night Scot football game. That night began 30 years of service to HPHS as the team doctor. Dr. Webb attended all home and away games, working to support the teams, student athletes and coaches. Dr. Webb served as the team physician under four different coaches. In 1969, Dr. Webb recruited Robert Rhoads, a freshman football coach, to be the first athletic trainer in HPISD. He serves on the Frontiers of Flight Museum Board of Directors, as the Capital Campaign co-chairman of the Theodore Roosevelt Association Board and as a member of the Turtle Creek Breakfast Club, which provides and delivers food and gifts to families in need. Dr. Webb is also a member of the Confederate Air Force, participating in formation and flyovers for military funerals, ceremonies and civic events.

2009 — Roger Blackmar, '50

Roger Blackmar's love for music began during his years at Highland Park Junior High School, where he and his fellow classmates formed a band called the Highland Park Hillbillies. After his military duty and college, he joined a Dixieland group called The Cell Block 7 that performed throughout Dallas. Blackmar and his band graciously performed for many years at the annual Golden Scots Luncheon, which honors Highland Park graduates who graduated 50 or more years ago. He has been active in the HPHS Alumni Association since its early years. In addition to volunteering in HPISD, Blackmar has devoted incalculable hours to bettering the lives of individuals and families who have been impacted by mental illness.

2010 — Susan and Marc Hall

The Halls are the first couple to receive the Highlander Award. They have worked tirelessly both as a team and individuals in support of HPISD and the Park Cities community. They have supported fundraisers for the Highland Belles and the Highlander Band, with donations of time and food from their family of restaurants. Mr. Hall has been a member of the Park Cities Rotary for more than 23 years and has served as president of the Board of La Fiesta de las Seis Banderas. Mrs. Hall served two terms on the HPISD Board of Trustees. She also served as president of La Fiesta, a board member of the Chemical Awareness Council and has been involved in numerous other volunteer activities.

2011 — No award given

2012 — Julie Ann Hudson O'Connell, '52

Julie Ann O'Connell is the perfect example of dedication to HPISD schools as an alumna, parent and grandparent. She has served as a PTA president and in numerous PTA board positions while tirelessly volunteering more than 1,000 days in the school cafeterias. O'Connell volunteers as a Living History speaker in district schools, giving students a face to associate with historical events. She also serves on the Alumni Association Advisory Board, on the steering committee for the HPISD Centennial Celebration and on the Mad for Plaid Grandparent Committee. Her community involvement includes serving as a church deacon and a Sunday school teacher, and she was named Mother of the Year by Park Cities People in 1986.

2013 — La Fiesta de las Seis Banderas

Since the formation of La Fiesta de las Seis Banderas in 1986, the organization has supported numerous needs and initiatives across the HPISD community. Hundreds of dedicated volunteers have given countless hours to raise more than $5.8 million. The Education Foundation alone has received more than $3 million in support of such vital areas as teacher and staff salaries, global education, the Tartan Endowment, school technology, drug and alcohol awareness programs, scholarships and Teacher of the Year Awards. The support of La Fiesta is critical to the success of HPISD and the many programs that make a significant difference in this community.

2014— Dr. Cathy Bryce

When she retired from her role as superintendent of Highland Park Independent School District, Dr. Cathy Bryce left behind a legacy of commitment and excellence that is appreciated by all who know her. Dr. Bryce, who served as superintendent from 2001 to 2008, made a tremendous difference throughout the district, thanks to her limitless energy, strategic thinking, gift for communication and above all her uncompromising commitment to each child. Upon her arrival at HPISD, she embarked on a listening campaign and was quickly able to identify challenging areas and set about finding solutions. Even during the most difficult of financial times for the district, under her leadership, HPISD consistently earned a Superior Achievement rating from the Financial Integrity Rating System of Texas. Dr. Bryce continues to be an advocate for increasing the standards of education for all children while working tirelessly to ensure that HPISD schools continue the excellence in education that is their trademark. She will be forever admired for her enthusiastic attendance at student competitions and performances, her deep appreciation for parents and community members, and her loyal support for members of her staff.

Honoring our alumni who served

In the late 1990s, HPISD parent Albert D. Huddleston whose wife, Mary, is an HPHS alum, offered to collect the names of all HPHS graduates who had served in American wars or conflicts and to honor them with the donation of a plaque. Huddleston had appreciated a similar plaque in his high school in Tennessee and was very moved each time he saw the names of students who had gone before him to serve their country and protect our freedom.

In February 2000, several teachers and students spearheaded a campaign to collect information about more than 1,100 veterans who had graduated from HP. Names were sorted by year of graduation and branch of service. A plaque was designed to leave room for names to be added over the years.

On Nov. 9, 2000, the Highland Park Alumni Veteran Memorial Plaque was officially unveiled. Air Force Colonel Warren Robert Lilly was the featured speaker. Col. Lilly is a 1951 graduate and was a prisoner of war in Vietnam for more than seven years. Just two days later, on Veterans Day, Nov. 11, a dedication service was held for HPHS juniors and seniors. More than 100 students whose relatives are honored on the plaque were asked to stand and be honored. As of 2014, more than 1,650 names grace the plaque.

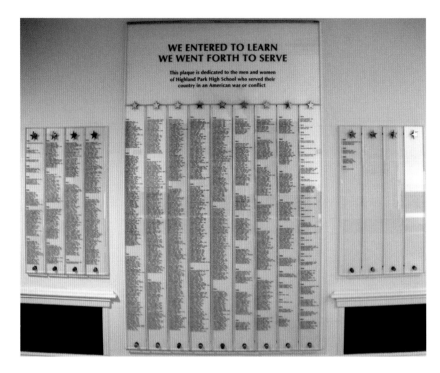

WE ENTERED TO LEARN
WE WENT FORTH TO SERVE

This plaque is dedicated to the men and women
of Highland Park High School who served their
country in an American war or conflict

The Highland Park Alumni Veteran Memorial Plaque, donated by Albert D. and Mary H. Huddleston, honors the HPHS alumni who have served in an American war or conflict. It is located in the front hallway of the high school.

The Community Members of the Highland Park School District
and
The Highland Park Education Foundation Gratefully Acknowledge

Albert D. and Mary H. Huddleston

For Their Generous Gift Of

The Highland Park Alumni Veteran Commemorative Plaque

Dedicated November 11, 2000

Their vision to recognize our alumni who served in an American War or Conflict has inspired our community and fellow alumi to honor and pay tribute to these brave men and women.

In addition to the gift of the plaque, Huddleston generously donated the funds for the production of documentaries in which more than 50 alums who are veterans of World War II, Korea, the Cold War and Vietnam shared their personal stories. In September 2002, the World War II documentary *Heroes Among Us* premiered. Then in May 2003, the Korean and Cold War documentary *In Defense of Freedom* was released. Finally, in October 2003, the Vietnam documentary *Honoring the Call* premiered. Each documentary features the veterans' memories in up-close, personal interviews. They have been shown locally on PBS and are used as a resource by social studies teachers.

So many HP alumni have bravely served to defend our country. Along with the Huddlestons, we thank them all for their courage and sacrifice.

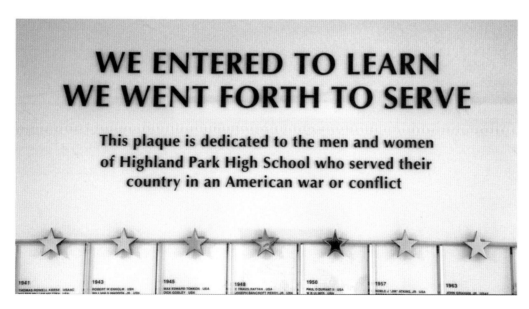

WE ENTERED TO LEARN
WE WENT FORTH TO SERVE

This plaque is dedicated to the men and women of Highland Park High School who served their country in an American war or conflict

ROTC

Highland Park High School initiated a volunteer-based Reserve Officer Training Corps (ROTC) program for boys in 1924. Within two years, the program became mandatory and saw immediate success. The HPHS unit won the 1926 state competition and was the largest organization on campus by 1928. HP had the distinction of having a senior chosen as the regimental commander of a ROTC unit made up of students from area schools for four consecutive years, 1938-41.

ROTC members were visible on campus every day, as a member would announce the opening and closing of each school day by playing a bugle and raising or lowering the U.S. flag. The band moved under the direction of the ROTC in 1927. The unit's popularity began to decrease in 1963 when the program was no longer a requirement for boys. Girls were eventually allowed to join the ROTC in 1972, with the passing of Title IX, but membership continued to dwindle. The once-strong organization was officially disbanded in 1978.

Top: *The ROTC band in 1925.*
Above: *Members of the ROTC in 1941.*

Left: *The ROTC Rifle Drill Team in 1964.*

Center left: *Members of the ROTC program in 1952.*

Top: *Practicing formation drills in 1952.*

Center right: *The A Company in the 1972 ROTC program.*

Couples

Lynn Ferguson Abbott
& Bob Abbott '64

THEN

NOW

THEN

NOW

Jenny Liebes
Castellaw &
Jim Castellaw '74

THEN

NOW

Liza Graham Ellis
& Jae Ellis '90

232

NOW

Anne Schaufele Evans
& Cole Evans '01

THEN

THEN

NOW

Leeanne Prichard Hunt
& Bruce Hunt '76

Couples

*Cindy Vaughan Kerr
& Guy Kerr '71*

NOW

THEN

NOW

THEN

*Francie Stevens Johnsen
& Lance Johnsen '84*

234

Sally Buckley Lane & Olin Lane '51

NOW

THEN

THEN

Betty Smith Morgan '48 & James Morgan '45

NOW

Couples

THEN

Kelley Rule Rather &
David Rather '87

NOW

Laura Hicks Rollins
& Bo Rollins '05

NOW

THEN

NOW

THEN

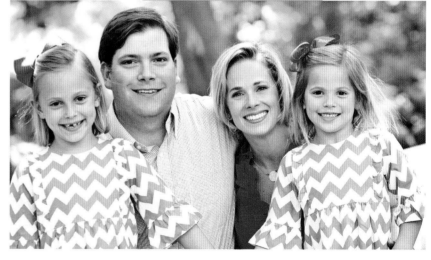

Elizabeth Thayer Speicher '95
& Drew Speicher '93

Multigenerational Families

Above: The Beecherl family is an anchor in the community and in Highland Park ISD schools, with four generations and counting.

Top right: The Holmes, Wallace and Winters families have three generations of HP graduates.

Right: Four generations of Flowers gentlemen (part of the Hunt family) gather at the barber shop.

Top: *Katy and Don Houseman gather with their children, grandchildren and great grandchildren.*

Left: *Seeing triple? Three generations of Scots by the same name — Jack Sides — have stormed the gridiron, carrying on the family and school tradition. The three are members of the Classes of 1957, 1988 and 2016, respectively.*

Above and center left: *Three generations of the Jordan family are pictured; four generations attended HP schools.*

Multigenerational Families

Top: *The Hallam family has three generations of Scots.*
Right: *Carol and Gifford Touchstone's family has boasted four generations of Scots dating back to Gifford's mother, Marjorie Touchstone, who graduated in 1927.*

Like so many HPISD families, the Teeple family's branches reach far and wide to include the Wrights, Tobins and Beckers, representing four generations of HPISD students. All those pictured above are part of the clan.

2014 UP volunteers carry on the long-standing tradition of serving food in HPISD cafeterias.

School
and
Community Leaders

Superintendents

Over the last 100 years, Highland Park ISD has had seven superintendents and 90 school board members. These leaders set the district's mission and make countless decisions in the spirit of carrying on the vision that has been in place for a century: to provide the very best education possible for the children of this community. That vision becomes a reality thanks to the

H. E. Gable
1920–1945

Dr. W. B. Irvin
1945–1954

Frank Monroe
1954–1974

partnership with parents and community leaders, including our Parent Teacher Associations, Dads Clubs and numerous booster clubs. In this section, you'll see pictures of our leaders in action, as well as lists of many people who selflessly gave their time to invest in the future of our children.

Dr. Winston C. Power, Jr.
1974–1990

Dr. John P. Connolly
1990–2001

Dr. Cathy E. Bryce
2001–2008

Dr. Dawson R. Orr
2009–

Board of Trustees

A. C. Bigger*	1914–1921
J. S. Bradfield*	1914–1933
M. Costello	1914–1921
W. J. Ford	1914–1921
C. E. Hudson	1914–1921
J. N. Kilman	1914–1921
J. A. Phelan	1914–1921
C. L. Kribs	1921–1930
R. C. Langley	1921–1931
Clarence Linz	1921–1922
V. K. Mather	1921–1925
Harry T. Moore	1921–1930
S. A. Myatt	1921–1934
D. W. Saunders	1922–1929
H. W. Bransford	1925–1928
W. H. Francis	1929–1939
R. C. Dunlap*	1929–1940
J. E. Lockart	1930–1934
B. B. Mercer	1931–1939
Dr. J. H. Black	1933–1941
George S. Watson	1933–1934
R. B. Whitehead	1933–1934
R. C. Buddington	1934–1936

Top: The earliest available photo of the HPISD School Board (1924).

Center: The HPISD Trustees in 1945.

Right: A Board Member congratulates 1974 grad Jim Hitzelberger, who would later go on to serve as HPISD School Board Vice President.

E. H. Flah	1934–1944
Mrs. W. E. Paschall	1934–1940
B. L. Woolley*	1936–1946
J. Cleo Thompson	1939–1945
George T. Hemmingson	1940–1946
Earl Jackson	1940–1945
Dr. J. W. Duckett	1941–1947
Mrs. Jack Elliott	1941–1947
Cedric Burgher*	1944–1947
George W. Hutchison	1945–1946
L. B. Merchant	1945–1949
Dwight L. Simmons*	1946–1950
Arthur Kendrick*	1946–1954
W. Perry McPherson	1946–1955
Dr. J. Shirley Hodges*	1947–1951
W. D. Prince	1947–1953
Mrs. Judson Francis	1947–1959
A. Sidney Briggs	1949–1954
Arch H. McCulloch*	1950–1972
Dr. John S. Chapman	1952–1954
George W. Jalonick, III	1953–1968
Dr. John S. Bagwell	1954–1968
Robert B. Moody	1954–1972

Top: Members of the 1977 School Board look over a report.
Above: The HPISD Trustees in 2000.

L. Preston Whorton	1954–1957
Jack Corgan	1955–1967
Clyde Jackson	1957–1966
Mrs. Ralph D. Baker	1959–1968
Walter M. Spradley*	1966–1984
Trevor Rees–Jones	1967–1980
Dr. Elgin W. Ware	1968–1982
Mrs. Robert S. Bush	1968–1977
Lee R. Slaughter, Jr.	1968–1976
Darrell M. Lafitte	1976–1986
Dr. John E. Eisenlohr*	1972–1988
Mrs. Duffield Smith, Jr.	1977–1986
Arthur Z. Barnes	1972–1981
Jack H. Davis*	1980–1991
Robert M. Reed	1981–1989
Frank Marshall*	1982–1989
Dan L. Beaird	1984–1993
Carolyn W. Stone	1986–1993
Judy W. Gibbs*	1986–1995
Sandra E. Snyder	1988–2000
Michael M. Boone*	1989–1996
Paul C. Lee	1989–1995
James F. Mason	1991–1994

Top: The 2006 School Board, with Superintendent Dr. Cathy Bryce.

Center: School Board President Leslie Melson presents HPHS student Natalie Rathjen with a university book award.

Right: Superintendent Dr. Dawson Orr and the 2011 Board of Trustees.

Brownie T. Watkins*	1993–1998
Robert D. Dransfield*	1993–2002
Hervey A. Priddy	1994–2000
Harry M. Hargrave	1995–1998
Guy H. Kerr	1995–2001
Jack D. Sides, Jr.	1996–2002
John W. Carpenter, III*	1998–2004
Elizabeth "Libba" S. Massey	1998–2007
Susan H. Hall	2000–2006
Houston B. Hunt	2000–2009
Jeffrey A. Barnes*	2001–2010
Walker H. Bateman, IV	2002–2008
John R. Bunten, Jr.	2002–2011
Douglas C. Smellage	2004–2010
Leslie L. Melson*	2006–
Cynthia W. Beecherl	2007–
Joseph G. Taylor	2008–
James L. Hitzelberger	2009–
Paul E. Rowsey	2010–
Kelly J. Walker	2010–
Samuel P. Dalton	2011–

* *Served as President of the Board*

Top: *Hyer students welcome Trustee Paul Rowsey during School Board Appreciation Month in 2014.*
Above: *Trustee Kelly Walker visits with students during a trip to MIS/HPMS in 2013.*

PTA and Dads Club

Armstrong PTA Presidents

1914–15	Mrs. Frank M. Gray, Sr.
1915–16	Mrs. W.I. Ford
1916–17	Mrs. J.H. Babcock
1917–19	Mrs. C. Hudson
1919–20	Mrs. William Bacon
1920–25	Mrs. E.H. Morgan "Honorary President 1925"
1925–27	Mrs. E.H. Nolte
1927–29	Mrs. Will R. Wilson, Sr.
1929–31	Mrs. Luther Jordan, Sr.
1931–33	Mrs. W.E. Paschall, Sr.
1933–35	Mrs. H.P. Edwards, Sr.
1935–37	Mrs. E.F.E. Schmidt, Sr.
1937–39	Mrs. Jack Elliott, Sr.
1939–41	Mrs. George Hutchison
1941–43	Mrs. Albert S. Briggs
1943–45	Mrs. George O. Wilson, Sr.
	(Mrs. Chester Cole)
1945–47	Mrs. J.N. Marshall, Jr.
1947–48	Mrs. Fred T. Porter
1948–49	Mrs. Henry D. Akin
1949–50	Mrs. Sheldon Lord, Sr.
1950–51	Mrs. J.L. Thompson
1951–52	Mrs. Howard Weddington
1952–53	Mrs. William B. Novak
1953–54	Mrs. Giles Miller
1954–55	Mrs. Jeff Hassell, Jr.

1955–56	Mrs. Ross Carlton
1956–57	Mrs. Robert Atwell
1957–58	Mrs. Howard P. White
1958–59	Mrs. Horace R. Nash
1959–60	Mrs. R.A. Eichenberger
1960–61	Mrs. Blair G. Mercer
1961–62	Mrs. Ross Madole
1962–63	Mrs. Porter K. Johnston
1963–64	Mrs. Lanham Deal
1964–65	Mrs. James T. Pryor
1965–66	Mrs. Robert Shuey, Jr.

Left: Mrs. Frank Mitchell Gray, the first PTA president in HPISD's history.

Above: The 2013–14 PTA presidents and presidents–elect with the HPISD leadership team.

1966–67	Mrs. Tom M. Matthews	1979–80	Mrs. Raymond O'Connell	1992–93	Mrs. Bobby Cheney
1967–68	Mrs. Joe Gray	1980–81	Mrs. Bob Christopher	1993–94	Mrs. Gerry Storey
1968–69	Mrs. George S. Rice	1981–82	Mrs. Richard Means	1994–95	Mrs. John Beecherl
1969–70	Mrs. Charles Paschall	1982–83	Mrs. Mary Glen Aldridge	1995–96	Mrs. Tom Somerville
1970–71	Mrs. R.W. Thompson, Jr.	1983–84	Mrs. John Sharpe	1996–97	Mrs. Jon Sparling
1971–72	Mrs. Ralph Belknap, Jr.	1984–85	Mrs. Richard Baty	1997–98	Mrs. Jay Humphrey
1972–73	Mrs. John Eisenlohr	1985–86	Mrs. Buddy Nash	1998–99	Mrs. Rod Riggins
1973–74	Mrs. Bassett Kilgore	1986–87	Mrs. Bryan Marquis	1999–00	Mrs. Stuart Bush
1974–75	Mrs. Robert Shoemaker	1987–88	Mrs. Robert McCullough	2000–01	Mrs. Doug Shamburger
1975–76	Mrs. Lee R. Kern	1988–89	Mrs. Lee Fikes	2001–02	Mrs. Rob Evanko
1976–77	Mrs. Craig Canon	1989–90	Mrs. Tom Rhodes, Jr.	2002–03	Mrs. Julie Grisham
1977–78	Mrs. Jack Brown	1990–91	Mrs. Jimmy Irish	2003–04	Mrs. Judy Hinson
1978–79	Mrs. Alfred Reubel	1991–92	Mrs. Howard Fitch	2004–05	Mrs. Janet Carter
				2005–06	Mrs. Wendy Crafton
				2006–07	Mrs. Kathy Sockwell
				2007–08	Mrs. Gina DeBeer
				2008–09	Mrs. Amy Powers
				2009–10	Mrs. Rhonda Sargent Chambers
				2010–11	Mrs. Laura Nell Morrow
				2011–12	Mrs. Elise McVeigh
				2012–13	Mrs. Amy Bales
				2013–14	Mrs. Meredith Mabus
				2014–15	Mrs. Susan Glassmoyer

Mrs. Gray, the first PTA president in HPISD, meets with campus PTA presidents during the district's 50th anniversary in 1964.

Bradfield PTA Presidents

1926–27	Mrs. E.H. Nolte	1966–67	Mrs. Robert L. Cottingham	1998–99	Mrs. W. Scott Robinson (Carla)
1927–29	Mrs. Will R. Wilson, Sr.	1967–68	Mrs. Carl P. Wallace	1999–00	Mrs. Mike Massad (Sissy)
1929–31	Mrs. Luther Jordan, Sr.	1968–69	Mrs. Wm. H. Seay	2000–01	Mrs. Jim Ramsey (Melinda)
1931–33	Mrs. S.W. Nichols	1969–70	Mrs. John E. May	2001–02	Mrs. Ted Frye (Ginny)
1933–35	Mrs. Will I. Lewis	1970–71	Mrs. James E. Coleman	2002–03	Mrs. Edward D. Biggers (Kathryn)
1935–36	Mrs. T. R. Freeman	1971–72	Mrs. William A. McKenzie	2003–04	Mrs. Phillip Gray (Amy)
1936–38	Mrs. Carey G. King	1972–73	Mrs. R.P. Stewart, Jr.	2004–05	Mrs. Quentin Brogdon (Cynthia)
1938–40	Mrs. Homer V. Smith	1973–74	Mrs. Edward White	2005–06	Mrs. Mike Barnett (Jill)
1940–42	Mrs. J.E. Jonsson	1974–75	Mrs. Joseph R. Musolino	2006–07	Mrs. Richard Neely (Kathleen)
1942–44	Mrs. J. Alton Jones	1975–76	Mrs. Dan W. Stansbury	2007–08	Mrs. Sarah Clark (Mrs. Mark Iola)
1944–45	Mrs. R. Kyle Duvall	1976–77	Mrs. James B. Hudnall III	2008–09	Mrs. Walter Evans (Susan)
1945–46	Mrs. James T. Elliott, Jr.	1977–78	Mrs. Sam P. Burford, Jr.	2009–10	Mrs. Aaron Kozmetsky (Tracey)
1946–47	Mrs. Ben Griffin	1978–79	Mrs. Thomas C. McBride	2010–11	Mrs. Stephen Sloan (Vanessa)
1947–48	Mrs. Carl Phinney	1979–80	Mrs. M.E. "Fritz" New	2011–12	Mrs. Andy Jent (Amy)
1948–49	Mrs. Lindsay G. Jolliff	1980–81	Mrs. Edward Halsell	2012–13	Mrs. Ches Williams (Caroline)
1949–50	Mrs. H.H. Beckering	1981–82	Mrs. Robert Hallam	2013–14	Mrs. John Anderson (Nancy)
1950–51	Mrs. Phillip VanHorn Gerdine	1982–83	Mrs. Joe Boudreaux	2014–15	Mrs. Brian Hegi (Libby)
1951–52	Mrs. Paul Stotts	1983–84	Mrs. Richard Allen		
1952–53	Mrs. Floyd Hightower	1984–85	Mrs. Mark Schafer		
1953–54	Mrs. Weldon Howell	1985–86	Mrs. Tom Abbott		
1954–55	Mrs. Thomas Howe	1986–87	Mrs. Michael L. Briggle		
1955–56	Mrs. Dan Voss	1987–88	Mrs. James Houston		
1956–57	Mrs. H.E. Cannon	1988–89	Mrs. Kirk Woodall		
1957–58	Mrs. Billy S. Colgin	1989–90	Mrs. Frederic Scripps		
1958–59	Mrs. Robert H. Millwee	1990–91	Mrs. John F. Harper		
1959–60	Mrs. Edward Wright	1991–92	Mrs. Thomas O. Pearson		
1960–61	Mrs. James D. Hancock, Jr.	1992–93	Mrs. George R. Marvin		
1961–62	Mrs. Robert F. See	1993–94	Mrs. Bowman Williams		
1962–63	Mrs. Julian P. Barry	1994–95	Mrs. Jack Sides		
1963–64	Mrs. Erwin M. Hearne, Jr.	1995–96	Mrs. Rosalind Bell		
1964–65	Mrs. L.N. Sparkman, Jr.	1996–97	Mrs. Daniel P. Hooper (Martha)		
1965–66	Mrs. Billy B. Joiner	1997–98	Mrs. Lawrence B. Dale		

Members of the Bradfield PTA in the '90s.

Hyer PTA Presidents

1948–49	Mrs. Carey E. Parker	1970–71	Mrs. S. Louis Moore	1992–93	Linda Goyne
1949–50	Mrs. Carlton Lawler	1971–72	Mrs. Val Joe Walker	1993–94	Kathryn Cook
1950–51	Mrs. Helen Emerson	1972–73	Mrs. Kenneth C. Stephenson	1994–95	Leslie Melson
1951–52	Mrs. Herbert M. Davey	1973–74	Mrs. Sydney D. Carter	1995–96	Debbie Dickenson
1952–53	Mrs. L. P. Whorton	1974–75	Mrs. William L. Ballard Jr.	1996–97	Cindy Kerr
1953–54	Mrs. Harry A. Shuford	1975–76	Mrs. Allan Hall	1997–98	Ann Delatour
1954–55	Mrs. Dan E. Boone	1976–77	Mrs. Kenneth Hays	1998–99	Toddy Glosser
1955–56	Mrs. Jack Corgan	1977–78	Mrs. A. F. Mahaffey	1999–00	Stephanie Dowdall
1956–57	Mrs. Robert Swango	1978–79	Mrs. Arch Beasley	2000–01	Amy Albrecht
1957–58	Mrs. M. E. VanHemert	1979–80	Mrs. Rhodes Baker	2001–02	Connie O'Neill
1958–59	Mrs. T. J. Warren	1980–81	Mrs. James Gibbs	2002–03	Kristi Gittins
1959–60	Mrs. Wayman E. Register	1981–82	Mrs. Ronald Cresswell	2003–04	Jamie Moore
1960–61	Mrs. Wylie Stufflebeme	1982–83	Mrs. Terry Wilson	2004–05	Bess Brooks
1961–62	Mrs. Herman J. Ruppel	1983–84	Mrs. William H. Dobbs	2005–06	Tanya Foster
1962–63	Mrs. Jack T. Titus	1984–85	Mrs. John H. Washburn	2006–07	Kathleen Wallace
1963–64	Mrs. Robert S. Bush	1985–86	Mrs. Robert S. Addison	2007–08	Jenice Dunayer
1964–65	Mrs. Alvin D. Sears	1986–87	Mrs. John Anderson	2008–09	Katie Pedigo
1965–66	Mrs. Robert F. Ritchie	1987–88	Mrs. John E. Whiteside	2009–10	Shannon Womble
1966–67	Mrs. Carswell Cobb	1988–89	Mrs. Paul C. Lee	2010–11	Holly Philbin
1967–68	Mrs. Homer Patterson	1989–90	Mrs. Lynn Phillips	2011–12	Betsy Welp
1968–69	Mrs. Darrell Lafitte	1990–91	Jan Doggett	2012–13	Kelly Love
1969–70	Mrs. J. C. Turner	1991–92	Martha Conger	2013–14	Heather Molthan
				2014–15	Katherine Lewis

The 2007 Hyer PTA Board in front of the campus.

University Park PTA Presidents

1928–29	Mrs. Will R. Wilson, Sr.	1967–68	Mrs. Richard E. Gray	1999–00	Anne Fisher
1929–31	Mrs. Luther Jordan, Sr.	1968–69	Mrs. Frank H. Elmore	2000–01	Cindy Bruner
1931–33	Mrs. Cullen Thomas	1969–70	Mrs. John H. Hudson	2001–02	Barbara Daniel
1933–35	Mrs. P.D. Keagy	1970–71	Mrs. James Robertson	2002–03	Anne Mackintosh
1935–36	Mrs. Sherwood Avery	1971–72	Mrs. John P. Pingree	2003–04	Liz Grote
1936–38	Mrs. E.E. Leisy	1972–73	Emily Hoover	2004–05	Becky Everett
1938–40	Mrs. E.Y. Holt	1973–74	Martha Floyd	2005–06	Karen Keith
1940–42	Mrs. D.R. Gregory	1974–75	Martha Barnes	2006–07	Ann Pitman
1942–44	Mrs. L.G. Williams	1975–76	Betty Taylor	2007–08	Missy Rothwell
1944–45	Mrs. Wayne Gratigny	1976–77	Bea Humann	2008–09	Michelle Cox
1945–46	Mrs. Roy J. Weaver	1977–78	Peggy Johnson	2009–10	Elizabeth Whitehead
1946–47	Mrs. Arthur A. Smith	1978–89	Winnie Hamlin	2010–11	Becky White
1947–48	Mrs. J.V. Edmondson	1979–80	Susie Silman	2011–12	Treca Baetz
1948–49	Mrs. J.M. Lynn, Jr.	1980–81	Jane Ann King	2012–13	Stacy Kelly
1949–50	Mrs. Lloyd Messersmith	1981–82	Anne Boswell	2013–14	Dana Manley
1950–51	Mrs. Jack C. Cason	1982–83	Ellie Hutton	2014–15	Diane Swartzendruber
1951–52	Mrs. George E. Bushong	1983–84	Barbara Lischer		
1952–53	Mrs. Elmer Gessell	1984–85	Prilly Evans		
1953–54	Mrs. Raymond Rosoff	1985–86	Sally Hamilton		
1954–55	Mrs. John A. Heathington	1986–87	Sandy Ables		
1955–56	Mrs. George A. Peoples	1987–88	Mardi Myers		
1956–57	Mrs. George A. Dehn	1988–89	Sandra Cude		
1957–58	Mrs. Ves R. Box	1989–90	Kathy Brooks		
1958–59	Mrs. Walter W. Langley	1990–91	Carol McPike		
1959–60	Mrs. William B. Stallcup, Jr.	1991–92	Gretchen Henry		
1960–61	Mrs. Bruce Orr	1992–93	Mary Mers		
1961–62	Mrs. John W. Storey	1993–94	Karen McCarthy		
1962–63	Mrs. Jack Harkey	1994–95	Kari Wade		
1963–94	Mrs. Roland W. Porth	1995–96	Ernestine Haas		
1964–65	Mrs. James W. Hughes	1996–97	Mollie Newman		
1965–66	Mrs. Forest V. Sorrels	1997–98	Rita Clinton		
1966–67	Mrs. William Record	1998–99	Janny Strickland		

UP Principal Dr. Rodney Pirtle passes the gavel to the incoming PTA president.

Highland Park Junior High PTA Presidents

1931–32	Mrs. R.C. Dunlap	1946–47	Mrs. Paul K. Cash	1958–59	Mrs. William Groth
1933–35	Mrs. A.V. Cockrell	1947–48	Mrs. B.T. Geron	1959–60	Mrs. A.J. Kutner
1935–37	Mrs. H.L. Pritchett	1948–49	Mrs. J.D. Francis	1960–61	Mrs. W.J. Dickey
1937–38	Mrs. Bentley Young	1949–50	Mrs. Lois E. Dolch	1961–62	Mrs. James H. Merritt
1938–38	Mrs. John R. Beall	1950–51	Mrs. Robert Webb	1962–63	Mrs. John Graham
1938–39	Mrs. Will C. Jones	1951–52	Mrs. John Rogers	1963–64	Mrs. Curtis Horn
1939–40	Mrs. W.B. Ruggles	1952–53	Mrs. Alfred Matthews	1964–65	Mrs. Jesse E. Thompson
1940–41	Mrs. Howard Dunham	1953–54	Mrs. Jack Brown	1965–66	Mrs. Jack E. Eades
1941–42	Mrs. R.E. Rettger	1954–55	Mrs. Luther Jordan, Jr.	1966–67	Mrs. William B. Stallcup, Jr.
1942–44	Mrs. Felix Butte	1955–56	Mrs. John B. Bourland	1967–68	Mrs. E.D. Peters
1944–45	Mrs. Ernest Tutt	1956–57	Mrs. Vernon Coe	1968–69	Mrs. James T. Pryor
1945–46	Mrs. B.C. Jefferson	1957–58	Mrs. Willis Lea, Jr.		

The Highland Park Junior High School PTA Board in 1968.

Highland Park Middle School PTA Presidents

1969–70	Mrs. Wm H. Hitzelberger, Jr.
1970–71	Mrs. S.G. Shaffer, Jr.
1971–71	Mrs. Marvin S. Sloman
1972–73	Mrs. Carlton Cranor

Arch H. McCulloch Middle School PTA Presidents

1973–74	Mrs. W.R. Goff (Joan)	1981–82	Mrs. R.R. Neal Bright (Becky)	1988–89	Mrs. Richard Slaven (Bettye)
1974–75	Mrs. Duffield Smith, Jr. (Ann)	1982–83	Mrs. Steve Mahood (Lee)	1989–90	Mrs. Robert Addison (Cappie)
1975–76	Mrs. James A. Rodgers (Carolyn)	1983–84	Mrs. David Kennington (Dorothy)	1990–91	Mrs. Michael M. Boone (Marla)
1976–77	Mrs. Walter Lightbourn (Beverly)	1984–85	Mrs. Berry Carter, Jr. (Sondra)	1991–92	Mrs. Bennett Cervin (Barbara)
1977–78	Mrs. T. French Snelling (Kitty)	1985–86	Mrs. James A. Gibbs (Judy)	1992–93	Mrs. Tom Watkins (Brownie)
1978–79	Mrs. Angelo S. Chantillis (Zoe)	1986–87	Mrs. Roy A. Kull, Jr. (Susan)	1993–94	Mrs. Jeff Swope (Ann)
1979–80	Mrs. Dan Stanbury (Joan)	1987–88	Mrs. Slayden Diehl (Carol)	1994–95	Mrs. Mark Aldredge (Laurie)
1980–81	Mrs. Allen W. Taylor (Sybil)				

Arch H. McCulloch Intermediate School PTA Presidents

1995–96	Mrs. Nick Meindl (Amy)	2002–03	Mrs. Scott Burford (Paula)	2009–10	Mrs. John McPherson (Anne)
1996–97	Mrs. Rod Sager (Ginger)	2003–04	Mrs. Joseph Taylor (Mary)	2010–11	Mrs. Dean McSherry (Susan)
1997–98	Mrs. Art Harding (Cindy)	2004–05	Mrs. Tom Stewart (Tricia)	2011–12	Mrs. Mike Walsh (Laura)
1998–99	Mrs. Jim Duncan (Rita)	2005–06	Mrs. William Washington (Marty)	2012–13	Mrs. Kurt Robertson (Carol)
1999–00	Mrs. David Gibbons (Mary Lou)	2006–07	Mrs. Houston Holmes (Sheila)	2013–14	Mrs. Rob Kibby (Leslie)
2000–01	Mrs. Bob Shaw (Ann)	2007–08	Mrs. Steve Utley (Melissa)	2014–15	Mrs. Bronson Stocker (Lynn)
2001–02	Mrs. David Bass (Jayne)	2008–09	Mrs. Steve Meier (Mary)		

Highland Park Middle School PTA Presidents

1995–96	Mrs. Tom Boone (Cordelia)	2002–03	Mrs. Gary Clark (Beth)	2009–10	Mrs. William F. Davis (Amy)
1996–97	Mrs. Marc Hall (Susan)	2003–04	Mrs. Patrick Jenevein (Kathy)	2010–11	Mrs. Jay Looney (Cynthia)
1997–98	Mrs. George Conant (Leslie)	2004–05	Ms. Pam Brock	2011–12	Mrs. Eric Nelson (Christi)
1998–99	Mrs. Bill Knapp (Gail)	2005–06	Mrs. John Livingston (Julie)	2012–13	Mrs. Prater Monning (Nancy)
1999–00	Mrs. Robert Sillers (Judy)	2006–07	Mrs. Paul Michaels (Lee)	2013–14	Mrs. J.R. Thomas (Natalie)
2000–01	Mrs. George Bedell (Karen)	2007–08	Mrs. Forest Felvey (Beth)	2014–15	Mrs. Craig Humphrey (Sue)
2001–02	Mrs. Dan Cheney (Kathleen)	2008–09	Mrs. Sam Dalton (Carol)		

Highland Park High School PTA Presidents

1931–33	Mrs. R.C. Dunlap	1968–69	Mrs. Robert L. Manning	1998–99	Anne Leary
1933–35	Mrs. A.V. Cockrell	1969–70	Mrs. John B. Jones	1999–00	Gretchen Henry
1935–37	Mrs. H.L. Pritchett	1970–71	Mrs. A.D. Sears	2000–01	Laurie Harper
1937–39	Mrs. Bentley Young	1971–72	Mrs. George A. Filak	2001–02	Margie Bankhead
1939–41	Mrs. A.A. Rowland	1972–73	Mrs. Addison A. Newport	2002–03	Cheryl Sargent
1941–42	Mrs. R.W. Roessler	1973–74	Mrs. James T. Pryor	2003–04	Lynn Lemon
1942–43	Mrs. Frank H. Garrott	1974–75	Mrs. Millard B. Jumper	2004–05	Nancy Williams
1943–44	Mrs. D.D. Redman	1974–75	Mrs. H.E. Patterson	2005–06	Barbara McKenzie
1944–46	Mrs. Ben Ball	1975–76	Mrs. James C. Allums	2006–07	Cindy Kerr
1946–47	Mrs. Tom Dees	1976–77	Mrs. W. Richard Davis	2007–08	Martha Sheeder
1947–48	Mrs. George W. Hutchison	1977–78	Mrs. R. Douglas Coffin	2008–09	Emily Deutscher
1948–49	Mrs. J. D. Ashby	1978–79	Mrs. Wendell A. Jones	2009–10	Annette Vaughan
1949–50	Mrs. Sam McCorkle	1979–80	Mrs. Peter S. Chantillis	2010–11	Jenifer Cody
1950–51	Mrs. Gordon McFarland	1980–81	Mrs. G. Douglas Gill	2011–12	Suzanne Laidlaw
1951–52	Mrs. G.R. Oglesby	1981–82	Mrs. Water Lightbourn, Jr.	2012–13	Susanna Ogden
1952–53	Mrs. Kelly Brown	1982–83	Mrs. S. Louis Moore, Jr.	2013–14	Eloise Meachum
1953–54	Mrs. R.J. Price	1983–84	Mrs. Robert Floyd	2014–15	Gina Culpepper
1954–55	Mrs. Dan C. Williams	1984–85	Mrs. Sam P. Burford, Jr.		
1955–56	Mrs. J.D. Vanderwoude	1985–86	Mrs. Frank E. McLain		
1956–57	Mrs. Paul Stotts	1986–87	Mrs. Robert M. Reed		
1957–58	Mrs. Hugh Peterson	1987–88	Mrs. Stephen C. Mahood		
1958–59	Mrs. J.F. Chambers, Jr.	1988–89	Mrs. William J. Goodwin		
1959–60	Mrs. Curtis Sanford	1989–90	Mrs. Herb Story		
1960–61	Mrs. Frederick Burnett	1990–91	Mrs. Jim Cochran		
1961–62	Mrs. A.J. Kutner	1991–92	Mrs. W. Philmore Evans, III		
1962–63	Mrs. Donald Bowles	1992–93	Nancy Egan		
1963–64	Mrs. Dean Kipp	1993–94	Jane Morrill		
1964–65	Mrs. H.L. Morrison	1994–95	Mary Montgomery		
1965–66	Mrs. Morris Harrell	1995–96	Anne Monning		
1966–67	Mrs. S.M. Mims	1996–97	Carol Mason		
1967–68	Mrs. Felix B. Goldman, Jr.	1997–98	Betty Martin		

Members of the HPHS PTA listen during a meeting in 1969.

Central Dads Club Presidents

1987–88	Bunker Sands
1988–89	Jeff Swope
1989–90	Guy Griffeth
1990–91	Paul Bell
1991–92	Bobby Lyle
1992–93	Walker Bateman
1993–94	Robbie Briggs
1994–95	Tom Sabin
1995–96	Scott Ragland
1996–97	Lon Houseman
1997–98	Jeff Barnes
1998–99	Bob Delk
1999–00	Mike Loftis
2000–01	Jon Skidmore
2001–02	Walt Humann
2002–03	Bill Koch
2003–04	Barry Bowden
2004–05	Randy Reid
2005–06	John Graham
2006–07	Raymond J. Kane
2007–08	James F. Williams
2008–09	F. Stephen Brooks
2009–10	Michael Fogarty
2010–11	Hugh Stephenson
2011–12	Brent Hudspeth
2012–13	John Hall
2013–14	Lee Wagner

Left: *Middle School dads prepare a tasty cookout in 1989.*

Top: *The Central Dads Club has hosted an annual golf tournament since 1991, which has raised more than $2 million for the district.*

Above: *Hyer dads working the lunch line in 1993.*

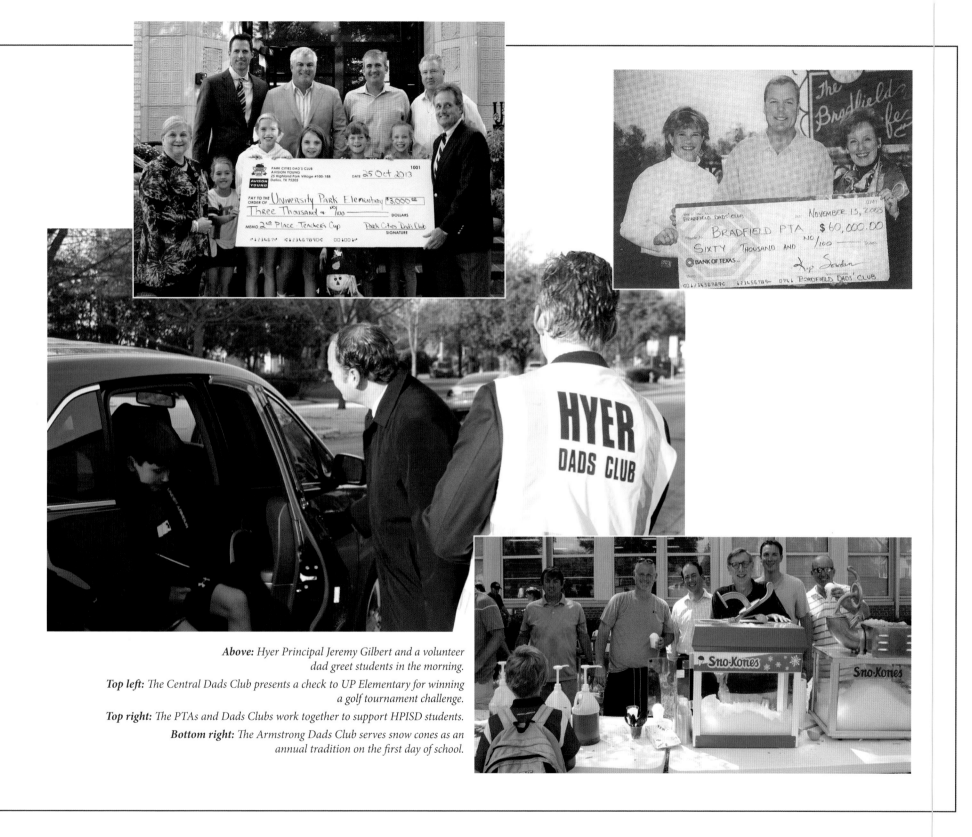

Above: Hyer Principal Jeremy Gilbert and a volunteer
dad greet students in the morning.

Top left: The Central Dads Club presents a check to UP Elementary for winning
a golf tournament challenge.

Top right: The PTAs and Dads Clubs work together to support HPISD students.

Bottom right: The Armstrong Dads Club serves snow cones as an
annual tradition on the first day of school.

Parent Volunteers

Left: *McCulloch Middle School cafeteria volunteers in 1989.*

Far left: *A middle school cafeteria volunteer prepares a sandwich in 1982.*

Top left: *Parents running the cafeteria cash register at Armstrong in the '80s.*

Top right: *Volunteers at Hyer's Field Day in 1989.*

Above: *Bradfield volunteers are ready to help in 2003.*

Below: *Armstrong dads dish out dessert.*

Left: *Parents running the HPHS supply room in 2011.*

Center left: *MIS/HPMS Principal Dr. Laurie Hitzelberger and her PTA presidents and presidents–elect celebrate the opening of the remodeled cafeteria in 2014.*

Top left: *Hyer dads work up a sweat in 1997.*

Top right: *Students and parents alike enjoy lunchtime.*

Above: *An Armstrong dad is happy to work the cafeteria cash register in 2014.*

Highland Park Education Foundation

Mission

The Highland Park Education Foundation seeks resources to preserve and enrich the tradition of quality in the Highland Park Independent School District.

Incorporated as a nonprofit in 1984, the Highland Park ISD Education Foundation exists to support quality education in the Highland Park Independent School District, currently serving more than 7,000 students. The Foundation benefited from the visionary leadership of George Connell, Judy Gibbs, Jack Hammack, Darrell Lafitte, Charles Seay, Walter Spradley and Don Williams as founding members. Today, a 30–member board governs the organization, and an advisory board of 25 members provides guidance concerning various Foundation activities.

For the first 10 years, Foundation projects were volunteer–driven, and annual distributions were directed to student scholarships, with occasional special gifts such as seed funding to start the HPHS Alumni Association. In the early 1990s, the Texas Legislature approved school finance laws mandating that the Highland Park ISD send a significant percentage of its tax revenue to other Texas communities.

Top left: The HP Education Foundation is governed by a 30–member Board of Directors made up of community members, parents, alumni and grandparents.

Top right: The Foundation manages and awards scholarships to more than 80 graduating HPHS seniors annually.

Other photos: More than 250 volunteers participate in the Mad for Plaid annual campaign to raise funds in support of teacher salaries, technology and programmatic needs district–wide.

The community responded to the pressing need, and the Foundation grew from a small operation to a fundraising powerhouse that partnered with PTAs, La Fiesta de las Seis Banderas, individual leaders and other community groups to help fund faculty salaries, teacher grants, teacher training and technology. Foundation fundraising efforts have grown steadily, thanks to the annual Mad for Plaid campaign. Gifts have increased from $17,000 in 1993–1994 to more than $2.5 million in recent years.

The Education Foundation manages scholarships, annual and endowed, established in honor or memory of alumni and members of the community. More than 85 scholarships are presented at the annual Senior Awards Ceremony each May.

While continuing to fund numerous programs and initiatives within the schools, the Foundation concentrates its fundraising efforts in three primary areas:

- Teacher Salaries
- Technology Upgrades
- Academic Enrichment

In recent years, a strong focus has been on the creation of a permanent endowment to provide lasting, reliable support for the schools. Together with Mad for Plaid, the Tartan Endowment provides critical funding to help bridge the gap between the tax dollars retained by the schools and the cost of providing an excellent education.

The Foundation currently has an endowment of nearly $14 million under professional management, with the interest generated supporting such areas as teacher salaries, the arts and continuing education.

Top: *Through the generosity of La Fiesta de las Seis Banderas, the Foundation is able to award grants to HPISD teachers to promote creativity and innovation in the classroom.*

Other photos: *Mad for Plaid is successful because of the work of its many committee volunteers. Members of committees such as the Grandparent Committee, Administrative Committee and the Sign Delivery Committee donate many hours of their time to supporting quality education for our children through this campaign.*

Alumni Association

In 1990, HPHS revived its Alumni Association to provide an organization that would allow graduates to keep in touch and strengthen their connection to the district. Art Barnes, a 1951 graduate, served as the first chairman in 1991.

Over the years, the Association has built an alumni directory, planned numerous reunions and established scholarships for graduating seniors.

In addition to class reunions, the Association hosts two large celebrations every year: the Distinguished Alumni Awards and the Golden Scots Reunion.

The Distinguished Alumni Awards program started in 1989 and was taken over by the Alumni Association in 1990. Since then, more than 50 Highland Park graduates have received this honor. Along with the Distinguished Alumni Awards, which are given to three graduates every year, the association also gives a Distinguished Service Award to a former employee for outstanding service and the Highlander Award, which is given to an individual who has made a major contribution to HPISD.

The Golden Scots Reunion began in 1994 to honor alumni who had graduated at least 50 years earlier. With between 500 and 700 attendees, it is the largest gathering of alumni every year.

Top: *1991 HPHS Alumni Board.*
Middle: *The Class of 1992's 20th reunion.*
Right: *Peggy Gray Marks, Class of '64, and Jenni Marks Scoggins, Class of '90, carrying the HPHS Alumni banner in the 1995 Park Cities July 4 parade.*

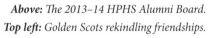

Above: The 2013–14 HPHS Alumni Board.

Top left: Golden Scots rekindling friendships.

Top right: HPHS class of 1941 celebrating its 70th reunion in 2011.

Center left: Don Brown, Sr., Class of '43, donated a collection of memorabilia to the HP Alumni Association.

Center right: Mary Smith Scott, Class of '34, receives the Oldest Scot Award from HPHS Alumni Director Jenni Marks Scoggins at the 2011 Golden Scots Reunion.

Right: Celebrating at the Golden Scots Reunion in 2012.

Ultimate Frisbee is a club, a sport and a way of life for its enthusiastic participants.

Memorable Miscellany

In every research project, there emerges a miscellaneous category full of facts and stories that simply don't fit anywhere else. Sometimes, these are the most intriguing tidbits of all. We are devoting the following pages to odds and ends that range from bygone traditions and activities to curiously unforgettable moments.

Above: *The freshman beanies were a longtime tradition at HPHS.*

Right: *Jerry Fullinwider discovered his love of music at a young age and was playing in a variety of venues as a student at HPHS and SMU. One of his groups was Jerry Fullinwider and the Southernaires.*

Below: *The first issue of the Manual of Standard Usage was first printed at HPHS in 1944 and has been revised nine times since. It provides tips on everything from efficient study tips to spelling rules and a list of useful Latin and Greek roots.*

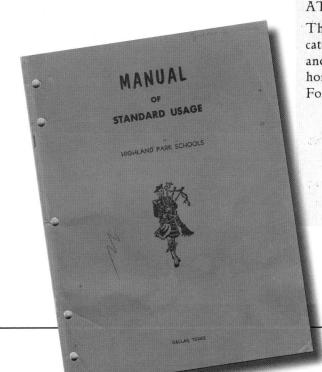

MANUAL
OF
STANDARD USAGE

HIGHLAND PARK SCHOOLS

DALLAS, TEXAS

Jerry Fullinwider

and the

Southernaires

Playing for the Music Festival Dance
Friday Night, April 25

ATTENTION: VISITING HIGH SCHOOLS

This fine orchestra specializes in youthful sophisticated music and is available for your High School and private dances, anywhere in Texas or Oklahoma, for a very reasonable cost.
For Further information contact:

Jerry Fullinwider

4724 Mockingbird Lane
Dallas 9, Texas
Phone D45904

Left: *The Linz and Everts awards were given for academic excellence.*

Below: *The UP Fire Department showed its community pride by naming a fire engine "The Fighting Scot."*

Above: *Doak Walker, a student in the Class of 2020, was named after his grandfather, football legend and 1945 graduate Doak Walker. Doak and the rest of the Walker family celebrated Doak Walker's accomplishments during a special assembly at HPHS in April 2013 hosted by representatives from the Pro Football Hall of Fame.*

Roger W. Blackmar, Jr. sent us this reminiscence of great times spent with junior high and high school friends, playing banjos, guitars and singing classic tunes. The musical brotherhood continued over many decades, leading to several bands, countless performances, and memories to cherish for a lifetime.

Ed Bernet and the Levee Singers.

Alumnus fondly recalls sharing a musical journey over many years with HP friends

Recently I attended a retirement party at Winfrey Point on White Rock Lake, a well-known and popular choice for parties and dances during my junior high and high school years. As I drove up the same old winding road and saw it, I was struck by the familiarity of the place after all these years.

Inside, the dance floor, the bandstand, the outdoor porch, the view of the lake, all virtually unchanged from times past. As I looked around I made my way through the crowd to the back which opened to a covered porch with a big double door opening to the outside with wide cement stair steps leading down.

No one was back there but me. It was quiet and I remembered. On these back steps Bob Irby, Dick Bernet, Angus MacDonald and I would play and sing with friends gathered around to hear us, as we often brought our guitars and banjos to social functions, always ready to do a few tunes. *You are My Sunshine, San Antonio Rose, Detour* and *Wabash Cannonball*, to name a few. Pretty soon the party was outside with us, instead of inside. "Little brother" Ed Bernet hadn't joined us yet, but soon would when he got to high school. Ray O'Connell joined later also after he transferred from Houston. Who could have imagined that that little group would spawn lifelong, enduring friendships and evolve into The Highland Park Hillbillies that as seniors wrote the song, *Open Up Them Doors and Let Us Outta Here*, and, at the request of the administration, performed the song over the PA system from the superintendent's office. A historical "first."

The group then became The Hilltop Ramblers at SMU that morphed into The Cell Block Seven who recorded an album for Columbia, to Ed Bernet's Dixieland Seven and continues to this day with Ed and The Levee Singers. Additionally, the original group participated in countless class reunions, Golden Scot luncheons, 35 Fourth of July parades, weddings, funerals, political gatherings and theological functions. Sadly two of the original four, Bob and Gus, are now gone and Dick and I are getting up there in years.

In the silence of the moment, I could almost hear someone calling, "Hey, Black, go get your guitar, they want us to play out back." I opened the doors, walked out and sat down on one of the steps. And we did a few of the old songs … in my mind.

These are the best and last memories of my days at Highland Park High School.

Roger W. Blackmar, Jr.
Class of 1950
2009 Highlander Award winner

The tradition of Powder Puff football games allowed girls to show off their skills on the gridiron.

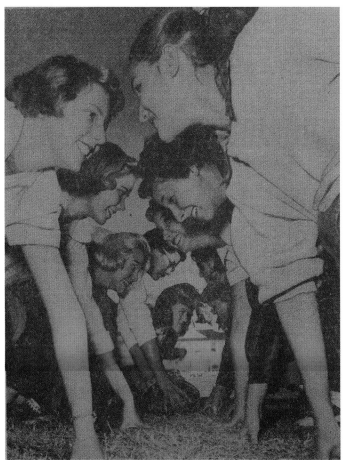

Top left: *The Quill and Scroll Club's initiation ceremonies in 1951. Founded in 1937, the organization's mission was to raise the standards of journalism at HPHS*

Two pictures below: *The sport of Tennikoit was introduced in the '30s as a tournament between teams from HPHS girls gym classes and grew to became an intramural sport. Scored like volleyball, a ring was thrown back and forth across a net until one side was unable to return it.*

During Highland Park ISD's 75th anniversary in 1989, the HPHS Student Council placed a time capsule in the school's wall. It remained there for 25 years, and on May 5, the plaque marking the spot was removed. Members of the current and 1989 Student Councils carried the capsule to a classroom, where they emptied it out and found the contents — a variety of 25-year-old athletic programs, newspapers and photos — to be in pristine condition. Above, 2013–14 Student Council leaders look over the items.

Left: *HPISD School Board President Leslie Melson, center, looks at contents from the time capsule with Centennial volunteer Kay Braly and HPHS Alumni Association Director and '90 graduate Jenni Marks Scoggins. Braly and Student Council leaders are planning a new time capsule to celebrate HP's Centennial.*

Below: *Class of 1989 Student Council members Sarah Huff Grip, Blake Cecil, Worthy Wiles, Claire Ellis Gentry, Patrick Lodewick and Blaire Burford Sherer proudly display their time capsule.*

This is to certify that

Cindy Vaughan

Has satisfactorily completed the first day of School.

After completing twelve pleasant and profitable years in public school, we look forward to the privilege of presenting another diploma certifying graduation from high school and admission to college.

Robert S. Hyer
School

Sept. 8 1959
Date

Newton L. Manning
Principal

Roma Craig
Teacher

Superintendent

Top: A marker on the second floor of University Park Elementary commemorates a cornerstone, which has not been opened since construction in 1928.

Above: Two information pamphlets from the 1960s for parents of incoming first-graders.

Right: A special diploma was given to all first-graders at the completion of their first day of school.

joining the clan

HIGHLAND PARK SCHOOLS
DALLAS, TEXAS

WEE LADS and LASSIES

Highland Park Independent School District
Dallas, Texas

The Ebby Halliday Family of Companies, which includes Ebby Halliday Realtors and Dave Perry-Miller & Associates, is the presenting sponsor of the HPISD Centennial Celebration, a communitywide block party on Oct, 19, 2014. Centennial Co-Chairs Bruce and Leeanne Hunt, HPISD Trustees and Superintendent Dr. Dawson Orr presented Ebby Halliday and CEO Mary Frances Burleson with a plaque during a ceremony during halftime of a 2012 Scots football game.

The hands of Virginia Proctor, Class of 1927, rest on The Highlander *yearbook. In 2014, Proctor was 104 years old, making her Highland Park High School's oldest known living graduate.*